THE GAMEPLAN
FOR AGING,
YOUR FOUR QUARTERS
OF LIFE

Mark A. Everest

With
Lori E. Everest

Contributing Editors & Lifestyle Factors Contribution
Susan Shapiro
Ronald Shapiro

THE GAMEPLAN FOR AGING, YOUR FOUR QUARTERS OF LIFE

ACKNOWLEDGEMENT

I dedicate this book to my best friend, Ed Lunney, who profoundly touched my mind, my heart, and my soul. During his long struggle with cancer he triumphed into spiritual health. As my teacher and mentor he was my inspiration for writing this book. I would like to thank my wife, Lori, for her ever-present belief in me. Words cannot truly express how much your support means to me. You are always there for me. I love you so much. And to our children, Marcus and Erica, thank you for loving me even though my travel schedule so often has kept me away from you. Whenever I think of the two of you I can't help but smile. To my parents, Dorothy and Rex, thank you for your love and commitment to me and to each other. You have provided me with a strong foundation and work ethic which I now use to expand my work with others. And a special thanks to Charles Tremendous Jones for inspiring me when I was but a young man, to follow my heart, find my niche, stay spiritual, work hard, and never give up.

Lastly, to all the people who have benefited from *The Gameplan for Aging*. You have taught me valuable lessons and have helped me to appreciate some of the greatest and simplest meanings of life. People have the ability to help each other, and in doing so, help themselves.

THE GAMEPLAN

FOR AGING,

YOUR FOUR QUARTERS

OF LIFE

TABLE OF CONTENTS

THE GAMEPLAN FOR AGING

The concept for *THE GAMEPLAN FOR AGING* is the result of over twenty years in sports medicine and rehabilitation. I have owned health and fitness clubs and have worked in sports medicine environments and rehabilitation facilities for athletes. I have consulted with and trained thousands of people, conditioning or rehabilitating their bodies. Some were ill, some were injured, and some were healthy and fit. Even though my clients ranged from the extremely fit to various degrees of being unfit, there was a common thread which their lives seemed to follow. Sometime, usually in middle age, they became aware of how their behavior affected their health, and they could visualize what might be awaiting them in the years to come. The healthy and fit people became even more fit and healthy because they were accustomed to a healthy lifestyle, and it was natural to just continue on that path. They knew that if they stayed fit throughout their lives, their quality of life would be much better in their senior years. The unfit people reacted in different ways. Some adopted minor changes and achieved a median level of health through their middle years, but spent more time and money either in hospitals or with more restricted activity levels than they would have liked. Others were able to achieve a greater degree of health, fitness, and happiness in later years than they had ever experienced before. But many did not know how to, nor did they want to, change their habits. It goes without saying that the quality of life these people experienced simply went down hill with time.

Differences in motivation applied to seniors as well. In 1993, I became a board member for the Department of Aging in the State of Pennsylvania. My company secured a contract to develop and deliver senior wellness programs at that time. Our objective was to work with seniors aged 65 and older to improve their quality of life through physical activity. As we all know, the older we get, the more set in our own ways we become and the more difficult it is to change our habits.

As I collaborated in assisted living homes and nursing homes throughout Pennsylvania, I observed the different attitudes of the people we were trying to help. One 75 year-old gentleman made a big impact on me. He lived in the same home his entire life where he had an active schedule. He enjoyed golf three days a week and had even taken up hunting, fishing, and other hobbies. He did those things that he had always wanted to do, but for which he never had time before he retired. Another 75 year-old man lived in a nursing home. He was taken care of by skilled nurses and spent most of the day in bed with nothing more to do than surf the TV channels for a program he hadn't already seen. I compared the quality of life of these two men, both the same *chronological* age. I was struck by the fact that some people are able to fully enjoy the latter part of their lives, while others live less than a fulfilling life. My challenge became clear. What could be done to maximize the quality of life even in the later years? Was it ever too late to begin?

While I worked directly with hundreds of elderly people for the project, I researched the subject of aging and wellness. I found that aging involves many factors. Some are "givens" such as genetics; others have to do with environment and behavior, things that we, as individuals, can *change*. Obviously, everyone ages in a unique way, but we can learn from understanding the aging process. We can then differentiate the genetic factors which might need special attention and planning from the behavioral pitfalls which we have created for ourselves. Remember, aging begins at birth, and the way we age, or "grow", affects the quality of our lives... especially in the last Quarter. (All of these issues will be addressed in the following chapters of the book.)

That vibrant 75 year-old gentleman, who is enjoying life to the fullest, is just one example of what a positive attitude and "preventive maintenance" can do for us as we age. What I mean by "preventive maintenance" is more than just taking care of our bodies physically. It's the maintenance of a good healthy attitude toward life. It's trying to prevent loneliness. It's trying to maintain a strong family foundation. Sure, there are going to be trials and tribulations, ups and downs, health related issues, and all the worries that go along with the responsibilities we acquire with time. These areas of life take significant work; sometimes so much that it becomes exhausting. But we can't give up. As my friend, Ed Lunney, taught me as a young man, we have to try until we die. If we give up, life is over. The journey will stop, and the outcome in the end can be a sad one... if, *and only if*, we allow it to happen that way!

THE STORY OF MY FRIEND ED

I owe my interest in making the most out of life to Ed Lunney, my best friend from my childhood through college years. This book is dedicated to Ed, and I hope it helps you as much as his example helped me. It is that example from many years ago, his confrontation with a serious challenge to health and well-being at a very early age, which has kept bringing me back to the questions I try to answer in this book. What can I do to improve my health? How can I live longer, be healthier, and enjoy my family and friends for many years to come? How can I motivate myself to make changes? These are questions that most people have thought about at one time or another, but many of us, instead of taking them seriously, put them on the back burner and ignore them far too long. Or we address them for a brief period, often because of some sort of health problem, and then slowly backslide into complacency again until the next alarm sounds. My own experience must begin with Ed's story.

Ed and I met in first grade during the course of one of those unprovoked boyhood confrontations, just pure machismo unleashed.

Ed and his brother, Paul, were surveying a vacant lot in Hershey, Pennsylvania, imagining who knows what: adventures, or forts, or baseball fields. Then I stumbled upon that same field with my brother, Rex, and territorial rights were at stake! We looked at each other, and without saying a word, began wrestling on the grass as if our lives depended on winning this very struggle. At some point, though, someone started to giggle. It became contagious. Before we knew it, we were all roaring with laughter, and from that moment we were friends for life. Of course, none of us had any concept of what "life" was or how long it would last. During those wonderful days of discovery, life seemed endless. The last thing we thought about was our own mortality.

My best friend, Ed Lunney (August 30, 1959 – March 12, 1982)
Ed's birthday and my wedding day, August 30, 1980

Over the years, Ed and I had the type of friendship that happens only a few times in most people's lives. Through our boyhood adventures, we became "soul mates". I think of a "soul mate" as someone you connect with spiritually; someone who thinks along the same thread; someone who will listen, understand, and care. That's the kind of friend Ed was to me. As we grew up together, we both played the same sports: football, wrestling, track, and baseball. Ed became an inspiration to me, not only because of the dedication he showed in athletics and academics, but also because of his integrity and honesty. He always seemed to set the standard. To me, *"he was the greatest!"*

Shortly after Ed enrolled in college, something entirely unexpected happened to him. While camping one day, Ed used his foot to break a piece of firewood against a tree. We've all done that at one time or another when we've needed to build a campfire quickly; usually nothing happens. But the next day, Ed became alarmed when he noticed that his foot and ankle were swollen. We all blamed it on the wood chopping. The inflammation and swelling seemed a logical result. He went to the emergency room that same day and described what had happened to the doctor. X-rays were taken but didn't reveal any broken bones. The doctor was a bit puzzled and again asked Ed to tell him how he hurt himself. After listening, the doctor seemed satisfied that the inflammation and swelling were a result of some sort of sprain. They put him on crutches, told him to take it easy, and sent him home.

A week passed, but instead of improving, the pain got worse. In fact, it got to be so excruciating that even the slightest physical effort resulted in such searing pain that he was unable to speak. Although trying to remain calm and continue with his normal routine, Ed sensed that there was a more serious problem. Then one night the pain spread to his other foot, up his leg, and entered his upper body. His parents rushed him to the hospital where blood tests were taken. Ed's white blood cell count was astronomically high. He was diagnosed with lymphoblastic leukemia and was given three to six months to live.

The news was devastating to his family and friends. Always the picture of health and well-being, Ed had led a vibrant and health-conscious lifestyle, and coupled with his optimistic participation in everything he set out to do, he had projected an image of invincibility. Ed was a bright young man with a great future ahead of him... or so it had seemed to those of us who loved him. We were in a state of shock, but Ed was not. Before long, at the age of nineteen, I found myself discussing death with my best friend whose life had barely just begun. I didn't know it then, but those conversations would have a lasting influence on my life and my work.

Following the diagnosis, Ed felt that he could develop a plan to fight his disease just as if he was working on a strategy to conquer his rivals on the football or baseball field. He also knew that he was going to be alright whether he lived or died. His faith and his optimism were unshaken as he began a grueling course of chemotherapy. He became very ill, but he got through the treatments, and his leukemia went into remission. All of our hopes had been fulfilled. Ed was getting well! His hair grew back, and he began exercising again. He was once again the picture of perfect health. Now he was even more of an inspiration to his family and friends. He was living proof that you should never give up.

Over the next year or so, Ed lived life to the fullest. He enjoyed exercise, sports, and camping just as he always had done. Most of all, he enjoyed his family and friends. It wasn't long, though, before he suffered a relapse. He came out of remission and became gravely ill once again. He experienced tremendous pain and suffering, but never lost his innate optimism. He never gave up. He maintained an incredibly positive attitude and outlook on both life in general and on his own struggle to conquer the disease. As his illness progressed and he became weaker, Ed developed incredible wisdom – wisdom far beyond that of the common man, much less, a man of his young age. He began to study the Bible, and that helped him to clarify the spiritual questions that arose for him. He knew that his illness would affect his family and friends, and his hope was that the experience would bring everyone he loved and cared for closer together. People began to gravitate to Ed. He was uplifting to be around. Local clergymen went to talk with him and were impressed with his outlook on life… and death.

Ed continued to battle the leukemia, and his battle was so successful that he went into remission again. Once again he became his old vibrant self. This respite was short-lived, however, and within a year the illness was getting the best of him again. He now shifted from fighting the disease to accepting the inevitable by looking at his life as a whole and deciding to live the final chapter in a graceful and understanding way.

I'll never forget the many weeks Ed spent in the hospital. I would communicate with him nearly every day, and when I would ask him how he was doing, his reply to me was always, "Don't worry about me! How are you?"

One time I asked him, "Ed, why do you always say that?"

He said, "I'm OK! I know where I'm going."

It took me aback. At nineteen years of age, I didn't recognize what it was that he was really saying to me. Only later, as I got older, did I understand. His wisdom and strength were phenomenal. During those visits and phone calls, he'd say, "Mark, do me a favor. Pray for the guy down the hall. He had a rough night last night." Or, "Pray for the woman next door. She was in too much pain to sleep last night. Pray that she gets some rest and becomes well again." He was far more concerned about others than he was for himself, because he was so firm in his faith.

Ed chose to discuss the realities of life and death with me during his last months. I didn't understand why at the time, but the older I got, the more I realized what a gift he had given me by doing this. I remember countless conversations with him on the beach in Cape May, New Jersey. We would talk about dying – two young men, boyhood friends on the threshold of adult life, knowing that one of us was not going to be a part of that life for much longer. Ed was very aware that he was going to die soon. Once he had accepted it, knowing that he had done his very best to fight the disease, he became comfortable with that fact. He spent his precious little time during those last days trying to make me comfortable with it as well. He talked about the lessons he had learned, hoping that I would benefit from them as he had. Surprisingly, I wasn't intimidated about discussing this subject with Ed. I knew that it was uncomfortable for most of our friends to discuss his dying because it seemed impossible to imagine life without him. His personality and his spirit were so strong that no one wanted to see him go. No one wanted to *let* him go; however, Ed, with his knowledge and his faith, was *ready* by then to let go….

Ed's life was far shorter than any of us expected it to be, but the memory of how he faced what is inevitable for all of us remains etched in the minds of all of his friends and family. Many people suffer the pain of seeing their children or someone close to them become ill and die, but it's difficult to comprehend if you've never been through it. People need strength, but they need to understand that this life is temporary. We need to make the best of it while we're here, and it goes well beyond the physical part of just living. Most of the trials and tribulations of life come from the spiritual part, the emotional realm of life. But if we can show the kind of confidence and faith that Ed showed, we have a good chance of achieving the peace of mind which allowed him to live every minute of the final chapter of his life to the fullest.

My friendship with Ed had a great influence on me as a young man, and curiously enough, an even greater influence on me now, twenty years later. Knowing Ed crystallized a thought for me, an objective, an intention that otherwise would have taken me years to see so clearly if I had not known him. Perhaps the most significant lesson I learned from Ed, which has taken on more meaning with the passing years, was a comment that he made over and over again.

"Mark, while you're alive, you need to try until you die no matter what your goal is. Never give up; persevere. Love your family and friends and love God."

This made such an impression on me that I wanted to try to make a difference not only in my own life, but also in the lives of others. So as I studied and gained experience in the fields of preventive health and wellness, fitness, and sports medicine, I knew I wanted to use that knowledge and experience in novel ways to encourage people and motivate them to compete with themselves.... to outdo themselves. Just as we can sometimes be our own worst enemy, we can also be our own best competitor. In order to motivate ourselves to improve, we need to be aware of the rules of the "game", and that's what this book is all about.

PART I:

LIFE IS A

JOURNEY

CHAPTER ONE
THE
GAMEPLAN
FOR AGING

Life is a journey. Are you prepared to go the distance?

Welcome to *The Gameplan for Aging, Your Four Quarters Of Life*. I developed *The Gameplan for Aging* for you - so that your life can be fulfilling and healthy. As a former athlete, who has worked in a sports environment for many years, I realize that all teams and competing individuals have a game plan to challenge themselves and their opponents. Without a game plan, their chances of winning would diminish. Without a game plan, *YOUR* chance for fulfillment and good health diminishes.

Corporations have a game plan, a "business plan", to acquire and secure a marketing edge. Their plan includes strategies for developing new business, retaining clients, increasing market shares, and creating improved products and services. Parents have a "plan" for their children. Such a "plan" addresses their education, their morals, and their understanding of life (especially as they enter the teen years). If children do not have some type of "plan", they may lose their sense of purpose and suffer the consequences as they grow to maturity. Likewise, older folks need a "plan", a financial and retirement plan, to manage and invest their money. They know that a smart plan will help them ensure a more secure future.

For many of us, managing our finances is far easier than managing ourselves. Managing personal behavior and lifestyle can be painful and exhausting. It is equally, if not more important, than managing that financial portfolio. As my grandfather used to say, "The hearse doesn't stop at the bank to make a deposit or withdrawal." And, of course, he was right.

Now, how about an aging plan for you..... a "game plan" if you will, that will help you manage your behavior, improve your lifestyle, and enhance your aging process. Most of us know what we should *not* do when it comes to leading a healthy lifestyle. Why is it so challenging and difficult to stick with a program?

Human behavior is incredibly difficult to change, especially as we grow older. With the passage of time we become products of our environment and of what we do to ourselves. For instance, most of us have tried to diet at one time or another, and we all know how hard it can be. That's because we are "craving" creatures. We crave what we are used to. If we eat a large amount of sugar or high fat foods regularly, we tend to crave them. You can crave exercise, television, golf or the Internet. How do we crave things that will help us age gracefully and yet still enjoy what we love to do? As you read on you will understand how you really can make change- and love every minute of it!

CHAPTER TWO
THE FOUR
QUARTERS

Twenty years a child;
Twenty years running wild;
Twenty years a mature man
And after that, kneel down and pray!

This old Irish proverb sums up what many people feel about life and what they can expect from it: twenty years of learning and growth, twenty years to enjoy the adult pleasures of life, and another twenty years of maturity which gradually fades into the twilight of old age. The popular wisdom of the proverb assumes that after age 60, life is a downward slope, if not a free fall, into a state of helplessness, loneliness, and depression. All we can do is pray! How many of us feel that way and just accept it as a part of the natural order of things?

THE GAMEPLAN FOR AGING, THE FOUR QUARTERS OF LIFE, divides our lives into four quarters: birth through twenty is the first quarter; twenty-one to thirty-nine is the second quarter; forty is half time; forty-one through fifty-nine is the third quarter; sixty-through seventy-nine is the fourth quarter. Anything after that, eighty and above is overtime! *THE GAMEPLAN FOR AGING* uses a very simple concept, *THE FOUR QUARTERS OF LIFE,* as a basic tool to analyze a person's life and develop a plan for preventive aging. It involves realizing that "aging" begins the day we are born. What we call "growing" in our first twenty years becomes "aging" in the decades after our twenties. Suppose we stick with the word "growing" throughout our entire lives? How about if we think of ourselves as "growing" until the day we die? How will that change in attitude affect our lives and our lifestyles? How will it affect the decisions we make in managing the *Lifestyle Factors*?

Plan your future health so that your fourth quarter is as good as the other three quarters of life. It is the quality of life that is important to consider. In the last section of this book, you will actually develop your own *Gameplan for Aging*. You will go through the *Five Basic Lifestyle Factors – Nutrition, Exercise, Sleep, Stress, and Attitude*. By following your own *Game Plan*, I assure that you can live your life to the fullest in your 60's, 70's, 80's, and beyond. In other words, in addition to praying (back to that old Irish proverb), you will be laughing, playing, fishing, golfing, enjoying friends and family, traveling, cooking, painting......whatever it is that you enjoyed doing in the earlier years of your life. You may even find yourself expanding your horizons by taking on a new hobby, learning a new sport, or embarking on a new adventure.

Almost every day new scientific and medical research indicates that many diseases and chronic conditions associated with old age can be avoided by making the right decisions concerning those important *Five Lifestyle Factors – Nutrition, Exercise, Sleep, Stress and Attitude*. I want to encourage, inspire, and enable you to make changes in your lifestyles now, so you will be able to enjoy good health in your later years. My *GAMEPLAN FOR AGING* is a simple way to motivate you to think about your own lifestyles and guide you in making small changes now that will bring about great benefits in later years.

Just as we accept the idea of "preventive medicine", I believe that we should embrace the idea of "preventive aging". It entails a redefinition of the concept of "aging", a new way of thinking about life. As you read on you will understand how I first realized the importance of "growing" until the day we die.

We Are All Players In Life

Aging is like athletics. Both are based on the clock. I've always loved that analogy, and I'll tell you why. Let's assume that we all live to be at least 80 years-old and that 80 is the end of the game. That's just an average taken from the current tables that a male's average life expectancy is 76 – 80, and a female's average is 78 – 84. Therefore, age 80 is our gauge for the "end of the championship game", keeping in mind, of course, you may go well beyond 80 based on good genetics and personal lifestyle. If 80 is the end of the big game, then from birth to age 20 is the first quarter of life, 21 years to 39 is the second quarter, 40 to 41 is half time, 42 – 60 is the third quarter, and age 61 to 80 is the fourth quarter.

You'll notice that a woman's life expectancy is a few years longer than a man's. The gap between the genders has closed quite a bit over the past 50 years. Women, on average, used to outlive men by a good 8 to 10 years. Why do you think this is happening? Well, whereas few women used to work out of the home, many have now joined the work force and have adopted some of the same behaviors as men. They are experiencing higher levels of stress, poor eating habits, sleep deprivation, smoking, and increased intake of alcohol. On the other hand, both men and women are living an estimated 13 years longer than they did 50 years ago. Medical technology makes it possible for us to control, and often cure, diseases that several years ago were a sure death sentence. People are more aware of the risk factors that contribute to reduced longevity, and physicians can offer medications to control risk factors such as high cholesterol or high blood pressure that can lead to serious consequences. However, accessibility to advanced medical technology doesn't always mean a better quality of life. Case in point – we just might be living much longer in a nursing home than we would have many years ago.

I have spent many years traveling in and out of the country conducting seminars on *The Gameplan for Aging*. I consistently ask the question during my workshops, "How many of you want to retire, or finish your game of life, if you will, in a nursing home?" Of course, the response is always the same. No one ever puts their hand up and says, "I do!" Both of my grandparents finished out their lives in a nursing home, and it always broke my heart when I would visit them. I remembered what their lifestyles were like there compared to what they had been.

I'm not trying to depress you. Nursing homes are a necessity for many of our elderly and sometimes even the not-so elderly. But as people age, they should not automatically think that being shipped off to a nursing home in their golden years will be a *probability*. One of my main goals with *The Gameplan for Aging* is to show people that by taking control of their lifestyles they can prevent finishing their game of life in a nursing home facility. So….. what this is, is a reality check – a gut check. Ask yourself this question. How badly do I want to win or lose the "game of life"? If you want to be a winner, which we all do, then you need to challenge yourself.

CHAPTER THREE
GENETICS AND
LIFESTYLE

Some people end up bald, yet others keep a full head of hair throughout their lives. Some folks develop very deep wrinkles, while others don't seem to have any at all. You can get some clues about how you might age by studying your parents and grandparents. Scientists believe that heredity, or the passing of traits from parents to their children, accounts for approximately thirty percent of the differences in life expectancy.

We have control over many things in our lives, but genetics is not one of them. Next time you're at a family get-together, take a look at your relatives, and notice the similarities. Are there a lot of tall people in your family? Is a cleft chin or high cheekbones a family trademark? The way we look is determined by genes. These genes give the instructions our bodies use to make our features: eye color, bone structure, and height. Genes also hold information that causes inherited, or genetic, diseases. Sickle cell anemia and cystic fibrosis are both examples of genetic diseases. Genes play a part in the changes in your body as you age. As people get older, they may have problems with eyesight and hearing, and their senses of taste and smell may not be as sharp as they once were. Your appearance changes as well; your hair may turn gray and your skin become wrinkled. Older people may slow down physically and their memories may not be quite as sharp.

So our genetic makeup (but not our destiny) is set at the moment of conception, and there is nothing we can do to change it. Human DNA contains thirty thousand genes made up of a long chain of molecules containing the codes for a person's inherited traits. It controls every aspect of our physical existence, including our growth and the aging process unique to each one of us. Genes control our tendency to gain or lose weight, our susceptibility to diseases, and any number of conditions related to aging. Our genes also control our nervous system and the way it works too. Many aspects of our personality and behavior, including our ability to *change* behavior, are also affected by our genetic makeup.

I don't want you to get the idea, though, that your genetic makeup sets your destiny in stone, because there is usually not just one gene that controls a specific trait or tendency. There are other factors that influence when and under what conditions genetic tendencies will be played out. The mere fact that we may have a genetic tendency does not mean that the condition will actually develop. Often, external factors such as environment or lifestyle come into play, and certain conditions can trigger certain genes. Although you can't change your genetic makeup, you *can* influence how it is expressed throughout your life.

Just by looking at yourself in the mirror, there is no way to know your inherited tendencies. Because you may look like your grandparents, or share *some* characteristics with other family members, does not mean that you share them *all*. Remember, we inherit one set of genes from our mother and one set of genes from our father, but there are thousands of genes and millions of possible combinations. So you see, there is no one else exactly like us. We're one of a kind!

There is a *Personal Gameplan* section at the end of this book. It will provide you with a plan that you will formulate. It will give you an overview of the diseases and conditions that run in your family. It will provide you with basic information you should know about your family. What were their diseases? Did they go for early treatment? Did they change their lifestyle habits or follow their doctor's recommendations? What was their attitude toward the disease? Were they optimistic or pessimistic? Are there examples in your family of people who have beaten a disease? What helped them do it? The more details you get, the more useful the information will be to you and to other family members whom you decide to share it with.

Once you have compiled this profile, what do you do with it? How do you use it to your advantage? Even though human beings differ genetically from each other by less than one percent of their total DNA, some people are blessed with a resistant and enduring genetic makeup. They may have greater strength and stamina. Longevity, resistance to disease, and athletic ability may be built in from the beginning. Other people, however, may be far less lucky. They may be prone to injury or disease and less able to enjoy the physical exuberance which defines the American concept of "the good life".

So as far as genetics go, we all have to work with what we are given and try to create the best possible conditions in which to develop and maintain good health and physical fitness. Knowledge of your family history will be helpful here since this will, most likely, involve changing or redirecting some personality traits or lifestyle decisions. If you have knowledge of these family tendencies it will be easier to create the optimum conditions in a plan that will succeed for your own set of genetic characteristics.

Remember, however, genes don't determine everything. Although we have no control over the genetic tendencies we inherit through our DNA, we do have control over our lifestyle. We can decide *how* we want to live regardless of the influences of environment (where we live, work, go to school), peer pressure, advertising, and family traditions. All these things can combine to take that control away from us... if we allow it. But hold on a minute! When we start thinking about actually *allowing* ourselves to succumb to all the nasty things life has to offer versus making some adjustments and living life to the fullest, why on earth choose the former? We want to "be all that we can be", not a bunch of "over-the-hill has-beens"! I know these clichés may seem all too familiar, but I would much rather my "golden years" *be* golden than tarnished with fatigue, depression, and illness....especially if there's something I can do to make it happen!

Let me share a few interesting pieces of information with you. When former US President, George Bush, celebrated his 75th birthday, ("old" and "over the hill" by many standards) he didn't just have a party with friends and family as one would have expected at his age. Instead, he went skydiving. Jumping from a plane, he plunged 4,500 feet before opening his parachute and returning safely to the ground. Now, to be able to have the strength and stamina to perform this fête at his age, or any age for that matter, he must certainly lead a healthy lifestyle in order to stay as strong and vital as possible.

I was recently reading a copy of *Growing Old is Not For Sissies II*, an inspiring book of photographs highlighting senior athletes, by author/photographer, Etta Clark. In it there are amazing examples of seniors who would put most of us to shame with their positive attitudes and excellent physical fitness. One subject, Erna Neubauer, an aerobic instructor who at the time of print was 86 years old, has it all in perspective.

"You can be flexible, active, and attractive at any age. I know from experience because I've been kicking around this playground for eighty-plus years, and I still move easily. I feel more into life, more caring about people, and more appreciative of myself than I did forty years ago. The secret is that I keep moving all the time. I have total use of my body. I am going to remind you: The first thing is that we should eat less, not more, and be more careful of what we eat. Keep telling yourself, 'I'm not getting older; I'm getting better.' We will never again be a terrific twenty, but we can be a fabulous eighty."

Another subject from Ms. Clark's book, Fred Ullner, a long distance runner at the age of 76, related a perfect example of what lifestyle changes can accomplish in your life.

"After a lifetime of pills, pot, alcohol, and poor eating habits, I finally wound up in the alcoholic ward at the VA Hospital in Palo Alto, California in 1977. I weighed 235 pounds, and my liver was the size of a football. I was also smoking two to three packs of cigarettes a day, and I was so short of breath that I could not climb two flights of stairs without stopping halfway up to catch my breath.

My diagnosis at the VA was acute alcoholism, with a fifty-fifty chance of recovery due to my damaged liver. I realized that this was my last chance to pull my life together. Starting at ground zero, I joined AA and managed to stay sober and feel better long enough to realize that God has given me the one last chance that I had prayed so hard for. However, even though I was not drinking, I was still smoking heavily, drinking ten to fifteen cups of coffee a day, and sleeping poorly. I was sober, and that was all that counted, but I was wondering how long I could hang on.

Then one day I got a book in the mail – *The Complete Book Of Running* by Jim Fixx. I read the book from cover to cover and figured it was worth a try *(to follow his advice)* and get out there and see if I could become a runner. I went out the next day, April 2, 1978, and I've been running ever since. I soon became able to run in 10K races, but it was years before I could run the Dipsea Race and the San Francisco Marathon, both of which I ran in 1986. That was the turning point in my life. I felt that if I could run both races and finish in fairly good time, I could do anything! Running is my life, because running gave me life."

I was impressed by these and many other inspirational examples of what a person can do if he or she is determined to employ the right lifestyle principles in order to enjoy "the good life" rather than sitting idle and watching the world go by around them.

For the purposes of this book, I have defined "lifestyle" as the Five Basic Lifestyle Factors: Nutrition, Exercise, Sleep, Stress, and probably most important of all, Attitude. These five factors, in combination, are a good way to monitor and improve our quality of life. We all have habits, hundreds of little habits, that make up the way we go about our daily lives, and most of these habits fall under one of the Five Basic Lifestyle Factors. A little later, you will find several chapters devoted to helping you adjust enough of these small habits to improve your overall well-being. If you have a clear enough idea of where your problem areas lie, whether they be genetic tendencies and/or lifestyle habits or situations, there are definite steps you can take to enhance your quality of life.

CHAPTER FOUR
"AGING VERSUS GROWING"

THE GAMEPLAN FOR AGING, YOUR FOUR QUAR-TERS OF LIFE, is based on cumulative day-by-day small changes. The long-term result of integrating small changes into the fabric of your daily life can turn out to be far greater than the sum of all its parts. We sometimes concern ourselves with aspects of the passage of time that are external to us (deadlines, holidays, celebrations, grad-uations, recitals, games), and we struggle to meet our responsibilities. However, we don't really take the time to think about what is happen-ing to our own internal well-being now or even twenty years from now. We spend a lot of time thinking about IRA's and retirement accounts and paying off the mortgage. But how many of us are will-ing to take the same steps necessary to maintain our health, fitness, and well-being as we are to planning our financial security?

When we were growing up, it seemed like we couldn't wait to get older. Now that "growing" has evolved into "aging", most of us no longer look forward to advanced age. Instead, we'd like to slow down the process. One of the most difficult aspects of the change from "growing" to "aging" is that we lose the momentum to do something better than we've ever done before. We lose the desire to conquer new territories. To combat this, we need to pay attention to ourselves and develop a plan to handle the passage of time.

How can we change the way we think about the aging

process and enhance it at the same time? We can't take it for granted. We have to begin to treat the aging process as something that must be thought about every day, like a checking account or a credit card, or, if you prefer, a plant that needs to be watered. The aging process needs daily attention from us. People who take it for granted are those most likely to suffer unexpected health issues as well as mood and attitude problems (which could affect their later years in a negative way). Many of us believe that we're invincible and can continue to go on and on in spite of the habits, pleasures, and vices that we've had for many years. Unfortunately, the aging process will catch up with us sooner or later, and when it does, it may be too late.

Aging begins when we are born, but we refer to it then as "growing". We think of the passage of time differently during the various stages of our lives. As a child, we "grow" and then begin to "grow-up". By the time the teen years roll around, we "mature". Only later, when we've reached our 30's do we start referring to the aging process. We might have thought that we were young when we were teenagers, but to our baby brothers or sisters, we were "old". When we reached our twenties, a person in his fifties seemed "old", but a gentleman in his eighties would consider a fifty year old to be a young buck! *We grow older.* That is really what life is all about. We start out in the world as a baby, and all the changes that take place in those first twenty years are seen as a part of a wonderful progression. But after a certain point in life, the path we all biologically follow acquires a negative connotation. Now "growing" is "aging", and aging is seen as a negative thing to many people.

When do we first become aware of the change? When do we begin to get the feeling that we've reached our peak and are now over the hill . . . or maybe even going down the other side? It can happen many different ways. Some of us notice a small physical change: perhaps a fine wrinkle, a few gray hairs, or a body part that now hangs a little lower than it once did. Maybe we're playing touch football one fall afternoon and realize that we're out of breath, when the year before, we could play just fine. Sometimes it dawns on people at their high school or college reunions. Remember the last class reunion you attended? You knew these people since you were young, maybe all of your life. How had they changed in the last ten, fifteen, or twenty years? Some people probably looked like they stepped right out of the yearbook. Others may have looked many years older than everyone else. Why? What makes some folks appear to age so gracefully while others seen to turn "old" before their time?

At my twentieth high school class reunion, a very large man approached me with a huge grin on his face. With a big, "Hello!", he picked me up as he hugged me.

"Mark, how the heck are you? Long time no see!"

Now, I'm sure most of you have had the embarrassing experience of knowing that you should, without a doubt, know someone (*because they seem to know you very well!*), but you just can't place their face... let alone their name! Well, I looked at him, and because I was embarrassed to say that I had no idea who he was, I replied with as much enthusiasm as I could muster, "Hey, Buddy! I'm great, how're you doing?"

"You don't remember me, do you? It's me, Jack," he said.

"Of course, Jack! It's been a long time," I said, still confused as to his identity. I think by this time, he was on to me, though, (probably the confused look on my face!) and I didn't want him to take offense, even though I was clueless as to his name. A few minutes later, after a little chat with another former classmate, I had figured out who Jack was. He was one of my old high school workout partners and had been a superstar in football and wrestling. He had received a full scholarship to play football on the West Coast and I had neither seen nor heard from him in twenty years. I couldn't believe how much he had changed! It looked like he had put on at least 100 pounds, and his head was completely bald. This normally would not have seemed like such a big deal, but we had grown up together in the seventies, so I had remembered him with the long flowing hair that so many of us had back then. I had also remembered Jack as one of the fittest guys in our class as well as one of the best high school athletes I'd ever seen. I was very curious as to what had changed for Jack over the years to cause this transformation. Later on that evening we talked, and he filled me in. He told me he had practically stopped working out. He was too busy, he said. After graduating college, he married, had three children, and acquired all the responsibilities inherent in a family: job, activities, house, and yard.

"I'm just not into it anymore," he said. "I lost my motivation after football, and with work and the kids, there's just not enough time left to work out."

Sounds familiar, doesn't it? How many of us can relate to Jack's story? We find our mate, we get a job, we have children, and we "*let ourselves go*" (don't you hate that terminology!). Jack and I continued to talk, and he filled me in on his successful real estate career in California. His life was great, he said, except he wished he felt as good as he had when he was younger. Then he began to poke fun at himself. "Mark, I've gained so much weight, when you look at the back of my neck, it looks like a pack of hot dogs! Hah! And look at this", he said, pointing to his ears. "I lost all the hair on my head and somehow it's migrated to my ears! Pretty soon I'll look like Princess Leia!" He laughed heartily at his jokes, but then sobered quickly. "Seriously though, Mark, I must admit that I am sorry I stopped taking care of myself. And truth be told - I almost feel guilty about it," he continued.

"Jack, you don't need to feel guilty. What would your old coach say if the team was losing? He would attempt to motivate you to turn that momentum around in favor of a win. Well, your life is much the same. When you stop taking care of yourself, you lose momentum and let 'aging' creep in and get the better of you. But hey, it's not too late! You can get motivated to do something about it now. Think of your kids and the idea that you can grow with them!" Jack agreed and actually seemed somewhat inspired. We've kept in touch since then, and the last I heard, he had joined a gym on the West Coast and was doing quite well. I look forward to seeing Jack again at our next reunion.

PART II

STORIES ABOUT

THE FOUR QUARTERS

OF LIFE

CHAPTER FIVE
FIRST QUARTER

My Daughter, Erica – An Interview
Clint Cullison – Youthful Courage

Let's go back to the four quarters sports analogy. From birth to age 20 is the time in life that we see the most dramatic physical changes. There are four key periods of growth and human development: infancy (birth to 2 years old), early childhood (3 to 8 years old), middle childhood (9 to 11 years old), and adolescence (12 to 18 years old). In this relatively short span of time, we evolve from a tiny person who cannot speak or even stand alone to a full grown man or woman with unlimited potential. It is quite amazing. If you are a parent, you know that incredible feeling when you see your child grow during this First Quarter of Life. Remember that adorable little baby who became the curious mobile toddler? Those first years were spent with an adult looking after them 24/7. As they entered the elementary school years, they developed in many ways; proudly showing mom and dad every wonderful new accomplishment. During this time, not only did they learn to read, but they read to learn. And the world opened up to them.

Progressing through the first quarter, a child moves into adolescence, perhaps one of the most interesting time periods. Actually, "interesting" is an understatement for this second half of the first quarter. I am currently in the midst of an adolescent explosion, with a twenty-one year-old son and a very social sixteen year-old daughter. As you may well imagine, for the past eight years, teenagers have been a very important part of our household. This is the time when kids become independently dependent. They are more academically, socially, and physically on their own now, but still in need of their parents' support and guidance. The teen years are a time of exploration, of testing their wings.

Remember when you were that age? Boy, I sure do. I don't know if I would like to go back, or even if I would call them the "good old days". However, one thing is for sure, having a good time was one of my main focuses in life! Now take yourself back in time. Think about your lifestyle then. How did you treat yourself? What did you eat? How important was your sleep? What kinds of physical activity did you do in gym class and in sports? How about the way we all carried on..... the party days? It's scary to think about some of the crazy things we did. Whoa! With the way my friends and I acted, I'm surprised I'm still here on Planet Earth! I'm sure you all have your own stories as well, some wilder and crazier than mine.

I talked to my 16 year old daughter, Erica, an accomplished singer, just to see if things were still the same as they had been when I was in the first quarter, over twenty years ago. There've been a lot of changes since then, and people are generally more aware of what is good for them, i.e. nutrition, physical fitness, and mental health, than they were twenty years ago. It would be interesting to see what my own daughter would have to say (considering the fact that I, as her father, am HYPER aware of what is healthy and what isn't – and am fully ready to admit that I DO preach fairly often about eating right, getting enough sleep, staying fit, etc.).

Mark: *Erica, what's important to you?*

Erica: *My family, my friends, singing, my health, tennis ,and having a good time, of course!*

Mark: *Just for the heck of it, if you could only pick two of those things, what would be most important to you?*

Mark with daughter Erica, age 16 1st Quarter of life.

Erica: *My family and my health.*

Mark: *Your schedule seems fairly hectic. Give me an example of an average school day.*

Erica: *Well, I usually wake up at 6:30 a.m. I do my hair and makeup, get dressed, eat quick, and leave for school by 7:15. School lets out at 2:30, and then depending on what's going on, I either go to a vocal lesson, play tennis, hang out with friends or take a nap right after school. I normally go to the gym to work out around 6 or 6:30, work out for an hour or so, hang out with my friends, do homework, and then go to bed around 11:30.*

Mark: *And are you tired in the morning?*

Erica: *Oh gosh, yes! I'm tired in school usually, too.*

Mark: *What about your weekends, what is your schedule like then?*

Erica: *Well, it's never the same, but I get up late if I don't have any early plans. I love sleeping in! Then, depending on what's going on, I either go to the gym or just relax with my friends. Sometimes I play tennis, work on new songs, or go shopping.*

Mark: *What about at night? It seems like you're never home, kid.*

Erica: *True, unless I'm having people over or there's a family thing to go to. Usually I go to parties and have fun with my friends.*

Mark: *Seems like fun is up there on your priority list!*

Erica: *Dad – you know this.*

Mark: *The First Quarter of Life, the" fun" quarter, okay, but how do you feel?*

Erica: *I feel pretty good. I'm tired a lot though during the week, especially in the morning and after school.*

Mark: *Well, you probably aren't getting enough sleep at night. Teenagers generally need more sleep than adults – 9 hours. You're getting approximately 7. Maybe you should try to go to bed a little earlier.*

Erica: *Maybe...*

Mark: *Erica, you exercise about 5 days a week. What motivates you?*

Erica: *I want to have a good body, and I don't want to have any cellulite. Plus, sometimes I just feel like I need it – just to feel better.*

Mark: *So the way you look is important to you.*

Erica: *The way my* body *looks is important to me.*

Mark: *And working out makes you feel better?*

Erica: *It makes me feel refreshed – especially if I've been slacking off for awhile.*

Mark: *How about your eating habits?*

Erica: *Mmmm... not so good. I like to eat junk food, and I think I'm addicted to carbs. I eat pretty much whatever I feel like eating... unless you're making one of your good dinners, Dad. Then I'll definitely eat healthy!*

Mark: *Hah! True, but you know, if you ate better on a daily basis, you'd probably have more energy.*

Erica: *True, I'll try. But truthfully, I'd rather eat whatever I feel like right now and then just work out.*

Mark: *You won't be able to do that forever. The way you eat will catch up with you eventually.*

Erica: *I know. I'm not going to eat like this forever, Dad. Don't worry...*

Mark: *So what's a good day for you? Describe a perfect day.*

Erica: *Ok... a morning when I can sleep in, then wake up to a sunny warm day, go out to lunch with a friend, lay out by the pool, play tennis, eat dinner, then go out to a party with all my friends. It would be a day that I would have nothing to worry about but having a good time.*

Mark: *Once again, having fun is high on the totem pole?*

Erica: *Definitely.*

Mark: *Here's a question for you. How fast does time seem to go by? From one birthday to the next, does time seem to go by fast or slow?*

Erica: *I don't really notice, but I'd say it goes by kind of slow. It seemed to take forever to turn 16.*

Mark: *I remember! It'll probably be like that until you graduate, and then again until you turn 21. After that, believe me, I doubt you'd be answering that question with the same answer. Time seems to go by faster and faster after that.*

Mark: *Erica, you have four years left in this quarter; you're 16. Apart from eating better, what do you think you should do now so that when you reach the next quarter of life, 21 to 39, you can be the best you can be?*

Erica: *Well, I plan on becoming even more motivated to do better in school so that I can accomplish what I want to do for my future. I also want to spend more time writing and recording songs. I definitely would like to eat better, but it's hard. I'm going to continue working out, and I want to become a better tennis player. One of the biggest things I'm working on, though, is keeping my stress low.*

Mark: *What makes you stressed?*

Erica: *I actually don't have much stress in my life at all. There's the little things that get annoying, but sometimes I get anxious over silly things. I've been working on relaxation techniques, and it's definitely effective. I plan on continuing with that. I think that it's a good thing for everybody to know how to do.*

Mark: *You're right. I use those techniques, myself, sometimes. How would you say your attitude is right now in the First Quarter of Life?*

Erica: *Great! I have a positive attitude.*

Mark: *What advice would you give to a younger teen?*

Erica: *Work hard in school and eat healthy. Stay active, and don't stress out about dumb stuff that isn't going to even matter within a week's time; just have a good time.*

Mark: *What would you like to tell parents who have a child in the First Quarter of Life?*

Erica: *Try to get your kids to open up and share with you. Get closer to them so that they don't feel they have to lie to you. That way they'll trust you, and you'll actually know what's going on in their lives. When you know what's really going on, you can give them advice instead of just telling them what to do or what not to do*

Mark: *So get closer to your kids with communication.*

Erica: *Right.*

Mark: *What else would you suggest for the parents?*

Erica: *Don't be too hard on your kids.*

Well, things haven't changed that much from 20-odd years ago, but kids today are definitely more aware of themselves, i.e. mentally and physically. As you can see, though, "fun" is still up there as one of the main aspects of the first quarter.

Clint Cullison – Youthful Courage

I'd like to share with you a story about a special young man. He and his family are dear friends of ours and have been through a lot the past couple of years.

Clint Cullison is one of those rare breeds of young men who is ahead of his time. He has a wonderful sense of humor and a wisdom about him which you don't often see in a teenager.

Clint and his brother, Dave, moved in across the street from us

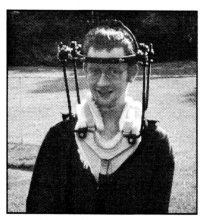

Clint Collison, with his halo.
July 2000

Clint at a party with his decorated halo.
July 2000

with their parents, Mary Jayne and Dan, when the boys were 11 and 10 years old. My son, Marcus, then 10, became good friends with both of the boys, and our families developed a close relationship. We shared many years of dinners, parties, family excursions, and a lot of laughs together.

It was interesting to see the development of the three boys as they grew up, and before we knew it, Clint was graduating from high school. His family was very proud of him. He had major plans moving ahead – a serious game plan for his education and a strong ambition to succeed in business.

The day of graduation was sunny and clear, and Clint headed off to graduation practice with three of his good friends, Stephanie and twin sisters, Jen and Amy. (Amy had been dating his brother, Dave, for several years.) As they headed home in the twins' convertible, their spirits were high. Freedom was just around the corner, and the four friends laughed and joked with each other. Suddenly, just minutes after leaving the school parking lot, Clint heard a tire pop, and the car fishtailed. It hit an embankment and flipped completely over.

Feeling as though he was in a bad dream, Clint tried to sit up, but found that he could not. His left shoulder was in excruciating pain. He looked up to see Jen and Stephanie out of the car, staring in shock and disbelief at the wreckage. They appeared to be unhurt, but as he looked in front of him, Amy lay unmoving in the passenger seat.

Again, he tried to get out of the car, but the pain in his shoulder was too much to take, and he began to feel dizzy and passed out.

After what seemed like an awfully long time, the EMT's arrived. They stabilized Clint's neck as a precaution and rushed him to the hospital. There, they set his dislocated shoulder and conducted a CT scan. He was then transported to the SICU Unit, and the next day, while his classmates attended their graduation, Clint and his parents met with his doctor to discuss the results of the CT scan. "I wish I had better news for you, Clint," the doctor said, "but your neck is broken. It's fractured at cervical one, five, six, and seven. I'm sorry." The news seemed devastating to his family, and Clint was frightened. He had a numbing sensation in both legs and his left arm, and he couldn't help but think of the possibility of paralysis. He had big plans! How could he accomplish what he had set out to do now? He wanted answers.

The doctor informed Clint and his family of the worst case scenario, which of course, they were already worried about. There was a very good chance though, he told them, that he could have a positive outcome, but it would not be an easy road. "We want to install a halo that will require an invasive procedure," he said. The halo is a metal ring that fastens to the head and attaches to a vest that is worn over the shoulders. "Basically, we'll screw the halo into your skull with four screws. This will stabilize your neck. You'll have to

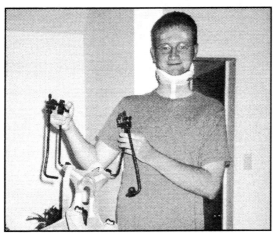

Clint celebrating the removal of his halo.
That was a pain in the neck!

wear it for 5 months." Clint visualized how the apparatus would look and what it would be like to deal with it day in and day out. "How soon can we schedule it?" he asked.

Mary Jayne looked at her son with tears in her eyes. "Clint," she said. "We need to talk. I know all this is going to be rough on you, but I have some bad news." "Mom," he replied, "What could be worse than a broken neck on graduation day?" With much sadness, Mary Jayne proceeded to tell him that Amy had not made it. Clint had a flashback and remembered someone placing a white sheet over his friend. At the time he had thought it was to keep her warm, but now it all clicked. Clint and Mary Jayne broke down and mourned the loss of Amy, praying for strength and healing for her family and friends, and especially for his brother, Dave, who would miss her terribly.

*"Strength does not come from physical capacity. It comes from an indomitable will."***Mahatma Gandhi**

Clint's game plan became redirected to getting well – Plan B. When he came home from the hospital following surgery, he had to adjust to virtually everything, from sleeping to bathing. His father, Dan, redesigned his bed so that he could sleep in somewhat of a comfortable fashion. He maintained a positive attitude, often joking about his halo. He even decorated it for parties just to add some extra good cheer. Everyone appreciated his good humor, and his wisdom reached new heights as often happens when we must overcome some of the curve balls life throws at us.

Through perseverance, a strong will, and a positive attitude, Clint made a full recovery within a year. He still suffers from various ailments associated with his broken neck, but doesn't let them deter him in any way. He went off to college and became an honor student. He placed second in the state of Pennsylvania in a business competition and fifth in the nation at the national finals, where students from all over the country competed in various business divisions. Clint never let this experience hinder him from achieving his goals. Always impressed by him, I asked, "What kind of advice would you give your fellow first quarter of life players?" He replied,

"First, never take your friends and family for granted. They are ultimately the most important part of life. Try to maintain a positive attitude, and don't give up on your dreams." I'm confident that Clint will be successful in whatever he ultimately decides to do. He was a first quarter of life player with fourth quarter of life wisdom.

Clint recovered from the accident.
Now a man on a mission. May 2002

CHAPTER SIX
SECOND QUARTER

MY FRIEND WALTER

The second quarter of life occurs between the ages of 21 and 39. Priorities change during this quarter, shifting from party-time and fun to career and "making it in life". Now, I'm not trying to insinuate that you should no longer have fun; however, during the second quarter of life, responsibilities change. Priorities shift. And what we could get away with in our first quarter, we may not be able to get away with in our second.

I was in my mid-to-late 30's (approaching half-time), and we were having a neighborhood block party, a shindig right in the center of the neighborhood, a festive occasion where each neighbor brought a dish to share and the beverages were flowing. Each quarter of life was represented that day on Morningstar Avenue with nearly fifty friends and neighbors gathered together for a few hours of fun and camaraderie.

Two doors down from my home lived a high school senior named Walter, a great kid and an exceptional athlete who was headed to the Naval Academy in Annapolis, Md. in the fall. Now it just so happens, wrestling was *my* main sport for more than ten years during my first quarter, so Walter and I would often talk about anything and everything to do with the subject: strategic moves, counter moves, and even psychological moves to use on our opponents. If you have ever been on a wrestling team, you know what I am talking about. Wrestling is a gladiator sport, one-on-one physical combat, and one of the most disciplined and physically challenging sports to participate in; however, wrestling is a young man's sport, and on that beautiful, sunny July day, Walter confronted me.

"Mr. Everest", he said, "I would like to wrestle you!"

"Alright, sure, Walter", I replied. "When would you like to roll around the mat?" In the back of my mind, I was thinking about going to the mat room at the local high school before he took off for college.

"Now", Walter said. "I want to wrestle you right now! I think

Walter Reynolds, graduated from high school, 1998.

Walter, graduated from The Naval Academy, May 2003

I can take you down and pin you!" This kid was very strong, a young man in perfect condition, but keep in mind; I felt I was in great shape, too. I worked out daily doing cardiovascular exercise, stretching, and weight training, so I felt pretty good about my odds of winning.

Before I knew it, all of my neighbors got word that Walter and I were going to wrestle. They made a big circle around us and began clapping and enjoying themselves immensely. This was unexpected entertainment! Standing next to me, my wife, Lori, nudged my side. "Mark!" she said. "What the heck are you thinking? Don't wrestle Walter. He's going to hurt you!"

I thought she was just being protective of me and I told her, "You've got to be kidding! I'm in great shape. I'll be fine."

"Maybe so," she replied, "but you haven't wrestled in nearly 20 years!" Well, by now, my male ego was a raging fire. Big deal! It didn't matter that I hadn't wrestled in two decades. I was bigger and stronger than Walter, and I could take him; I was sure of it! I started to get a few butterflies, but my son, Marcus, who was about 14 at the time, strengthened my resolve.

"Do it, Dad! You can pin him, no problem," he said. "Show Walter you've STILL GOT IT!"

Well, that comment chased away any doubts that still lingered – and any sense as well. I was now convinced that I should take the challenge. Walter anxiously awaited my answer along with all my neighbors who were chanting, "Fight! Fight! Fight!" just to be funny. My adrenaline was flowing, and I was back in Hershey High School's gym. I even pictured myself on the mat.

"Bring it on, Walter! Show me what you've got!"

Visualize this with me for just a moment. Fifty to sixty neighbors of all ages encircling a nearly middle-aged man about to wrestle a seventeen year-old first quarter player while they chanted "Fight! Fight! Fight!" I mean, this was quite a spectacle! The last thing I could imagine was for Walter to actually pin me in front of my son, let alone the 100 eyes eagerly watching. U-h-h – maybe somebody should say EGO?! My butterflies increased about tenfold, but there was no way I was going to back down now. I was taking this match very seriously. You would have thought this bout was for the state finals!

We shook hands, and the match was on. The first move in wrestling is to tie up with your opponent. That is when the two wrestlers lock heads together with their hands, testing each other's strength. Well, I locked up with Walter, and I got scared. He was not only strong, but he was also quick. His moves were fresh. I wasn't so sure anymore that I could beat this kid, and I began to feel old and rusty. My friends would never let me live it down if he actually pinned me, so my strategy was clear. The only way I could possibly beat Walter was to muscle him to the ground, put him in a cradle (which just happened to be my signature move in high school), and *hopefully* pin him. I began to apply all the muscle I had, using all of my weight advantage. We kept this up for what seemed like an eternity; Walter, wrestling like the nimble young athlete he was, and me, trying to use all my strength like a big WWF bully wrestler. Finally, through sheer persistence and determination not to make a fool of myself, I used every ounce of strength and weight and actually got Walter to the ground. I put him in a cradle as fast as I could and PINNED HIM! Wha-hoo! Victory! I was exhausted.

Walter, on the other hand, stood up, shook it off like nothing had happened, and said, "Good job, Mr. Everest. That was fun!" My son, Marcus, was beaming, and he put my hand up in victory just as the pros do after winning their wrestling matches. My neighbors were all slapping me on the back, and I felt like I was back at the old school gym with my schoolmates cheering me on to victory. Oh, what a feeling!

The next morning.... *Oh, what a feeling!* I could barely move. I felt as if I had just been beaten to a pulp. My head was stuck in an odd position, and I was in excruciating pain... everywhere. I fully admit that I was acting like a complete baby, but I didn't care. My moaning woke Lori up. She took one look at me and said, "I told you Walter was going to hurt you. Now look at you. You can't even move! Sorry, honey, no sympathy here."

Now, being in the field of sports medicine and prevention, I knew full well that it was not a wise move to wrestle Walter. But for those few moments of confrontation, I felt obliged to go back to my first quarter of life and duplicate what I used to do. I have to tell you, though, I learned the hard way what a mistake that was.

Later that afternoon, I received a knock at my door, and I could see through the front window that it was Walter. My first thought was, "Oh no, it's Walter, and he wants a rematch". I got up from my chair and realigned my head. In pain, but trying desperately to appear that I was feeling like a champion, I opened the door praying that Walter would not ask for a rematch.

"Mr. Everest," he said, "I just wanted to come over here to let you know that you surprised me yesterday. You still got it!"

To this day, Walter still has no idea that, though I pinned him, he was the actual winner. The moral of this story: when you think you may still have *it*, think again. Use the experience you gain as you progress through the quarters of life.

It's hard for me to believe the time has passed so quickly. It was half my lifetime ago that I was 21 years old! I remember my twenties as a time of exploration. I found my career niche during that period, got married, and had two kids. Life was simpler for me then. Yes, my ideas were big, and I had financial problems like everyone else, but I felt as if I had plenty of time to accomplish my goals. For a lot of people, though, the twenties are a time of frustration and rude awakening.

High school and college graduates head into the working world with thoughts of a "big" career and a "big" salary to match. People in their twenties, more often than not, find that the real world is a lot tougher than they had anticipated. Just looking for a job can be frustrating, time consuming, and costly. We've all been there, and you know that it's not unusual to send resume after resume after resume. Meanwhile, there are student loans to repay, household bills, car loans, forms to fill out, and normal, everyday problems to worry about. Of course, we all face these realities, but they are new to those in their early and mid-twenties. My son, Marcus, who at 20 was trying to make it in New York City, found this out firsthand. Whenever he would complain about his finances (which translated to: "I don't have enough money."), I couldn't help but say, "Welcome to the real world, bud!" He would just laugh, "I know, Dad, I know, but could you just tide me over 'till...." Well, no one ever said things would be easy, but kids in their first quarter can't wait to be in their twenties, and as Marcus found out firsthand, being in his second quarter was going to take a lot more work than he had anticipated. "Fun" is still important, of course, but has to take a backseat to getting a little more serious about life.

It can be tough to make it in this age group, but it is also a decade of great times. The twenties are a period when all the other ages envy you. You're old enough to be on your own, doing what you please, but you're considered young by everyone else's standards (except a young child's). You have the whole world in front of you, and a lot of time to get where you want to be.

It's easy to think that at this age there is no reason to eat right or exercise because you still have that feeling of invincibility you had when you were a kid. Remember that? We thought nothing could touch us, because really "bad" stuff only happened to "old" people, and being young gave us the gift of time. I recently had a conversation with my friend's daughter. She is 23 years-old and was very quick to say, "Oh, I don't work out. I'll do that when my body starts to look bad, and right now, it looks fine to me!"

Her girlfriend agreed wholeheartedly. "Yeah," she said, "I work, and when I have free time, I party. We don't get home until 3:00 A.M. in the morning, and then I usually sleep the next day until at least noon! I don't have time to work out!"

The truth of the matter, though, is that the twenties are a very important time to establish fitness habits that you will carry with you as you get older. It is much harder to start from scratch when you are older because your body is a lot less resilient. So, it pays to take the time for yourself, (and not wait until you "look bad") because the gains you make now may have an effect on your health in later years.

Although during your twenties you may not be all that interested in eating right and working out simply because you "don't look bad", most people would agree that many physical signs of aging really begin to appear during their thirties. This is when we begin to see those little wrinkles start to deepen around our eyes, and those laugh lines that helped us to look so animated when we smiled, sort of stay there now when we relax our face. For the most part, though, outwardly your body is not that different at 34 than it was at 24, especially if you are male or are a woman who has never had any children. Even if you are a woman who has given birth, it's not so much that you are now in your thirties as compared to your twenties, but rather the simple fact that your body has gone through the significant physical changes of pregnancy and childbirth.

However, though you may look pretty much the same now as you did a few years ago, those wrinkles and a little less hair notwithstanding, there are some definite, yet unperceivable changes during this decade of life. Our muscle mass, strength, aerobic state, and metabolism all begin a slow downward spiral. How many of you have said, "Gosh! I used to be able to eat anything I wanted and never gained an ounce!" To be quite honest, there was even a time many years ago when *I* used to down cheese steak sandwiches and donuts on a regular basis with no regret whatsoever! And not only did I not regret it, I didn't see any physical effects from eating that way. Now, in my mid forties, I have to watch everything I eat. If I ate like I used to, I'd blow up like a balloon. Worse yet, I shudder to think what a habit like that could be doing to my arteries.

So if you haven't eaten right and exercised regularly during your twenties, now is definitely the time to begin. But here's the hard part. We're really busy. I mean, *really* busy! There's a lot going on in our lives at this age. Many people have young families with all the activities that go along with them and a career that is now in full swing. These two things alone can easily consume the majority of our time. And not only are we super busy, but we're stressed, too! There just aren't enough hours in the day to do everything. What we need is a 30 hour day... or maybe we should just sleep less and work more! Nah... I really don't think that would do the trick, though the 30 hour day *is* a fascinating thought. Just think what we could do with an extra 6 hours a day! The good news is that, although we can't extend our day, we can manage ourselves better. This translates into thinking about what goes into our bodies, and realizing that making wise choices will give the right balance of nutrients to fuel our bodies efficiently. If you eat right, you'll end up stronger, faster, and have enough energy to do all the things you need to do in a day. Now comes the tougher part of self management... making time to workout. The thing is, you can't *make* time. No one can. What we can do, though, is choose how we spend the time we do have. We all make time to maintain our cars, clean our houses, and shop for groceries. We even make time to watch our favorite television shows. Isn't your health worth at least the 30 to 60 minutes a day it would take to go for a walk, ride your bike, or go to the gym? Think about it.

As you progress through this book, it's very easy to relate to the various experiences that we all encounter during each quarter of life. However, your personal challenge is not just to identify with the quarters of life, but to put into practice your own personal Gameplan for Aging to manage your life. Remember, it's all about the small changes made each and every day that, in return, will produce big gains and ultimately, that big win in the fourth quarter.

CHAPTER SEVEN
HALFTIME

DONNA'S STORY

In an athletic event, halftime is when the teams go back into the locker room to regroup. It's an interesting environment, especially if you're in the room with the team that's losing the game. I'm certain that many of you reading this book can relate to locker room talks. What does the coach say to the players if the team is losing at half time? Does he or she say, "Hey, team! You're looking sharp out there today! Let's keep up the good work. We can make a comeback if we just keep doing what we've been doing!" *Doubtful!* If the team is losing, the coach will try to re-motivate the players. He or she will take out the playbook and incorporate new strategies. The coach is trying to redirect the behavior of the players (behavior modification), because the team can't afford to make the same mistakes they made in the first half.

Aging is pretty much the same. If we don't feel as good as we can possibly feel, then we are losing momentum just like that sports team. Ask yourself a question and answer it honestly. How are, or were, the first two quarters of life? Keep in mind there are many factors that make up a good first half of life. Health is a very significant factor, but family, finances, and physical and emotional issues also play a huge role. If you've already passed that halftime mark, and are dissatisfied, ask yourself what you think could have been done to make things better? It's unfortunate that we can't turn back the clock, for if we could….. I know that I, for one, would definitely have made some play changes along the way.

When I speak to high school or college students, and I talk about halftime in life, they say they'll make their personal play changes *at* halftime….whenever that time comes. Right now, they're just having too much fun! Forty years old is a million years away. Gosh, that's OLD! And, hey, I agree with the "fun" aspect! Remember one of the mission statements of the first quarter of life? For most, it's "Party Time"! Why not? However, if you think about an athletic game, how many coaches would say, "Hey, team, let's go out and lose the first two quarters of the game today! It's cool! Don't worry about it. We can make it up in the second half!" *That* would really make the game exciting for the fans, wouldn't it? I haven't met a coach yet who wants to be losing in the first two quarters of the game. Why? Momentum! Once you get it, you want to keep it; otherwise you have to work twice as hard to make up for slacking off in the first half. Aging is the same. Capture that momentum, and once you have it, you have to work at keeping it up! We progressively lose some momentum as we move from one quarter of life to the next, and if we simply let whatever happens happen, without trying to make things better for ourselves, without pushing to keep that momentum going, we will ultimately lose.

But what if our momentum is in full gear, going strong – and the unforeseen happens? What if, despite all our positive actions, something occurs to totally interrupt our lives; something so major that we can barely function, let alone push to keep our momentum going? Life altering events happen every day. We think they'll happen to somebody else, but inevitably these things do end up touching our lives. My sister-in-law, Donna, had such an experience. Nearing her forty-first birthday, she discovered a lump in her breast that was diagnosed malignant. I have been inspired by many people over the years, but Donna is the perfect example of the type of person I admire most. In fact, she has inspired so many of us, that I asked Donna to write her own story to add to the *Gameplan for Aging*.

DONNA'S STORY

"When I was asked to contribute my experience to *Gameplan*

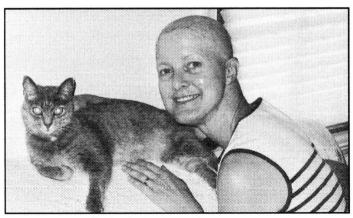

*Donna Reese, my sister-in-law, during
chemotherapy treatments, August 2002*

for Aging - Your Four Quarters of Life, I wondered what I could say that would motivate others. I went through a long and life threatening illness, but never felt that I was a particularly brave woman or that I could really be an inspiration to anyone. During my illness, I was very scared and sometimes discouraged. After reading Ed's story and knowing him personally, I knew that I was not the strong person that he was during his illness. I have always been a very patient and goal oriented person, though. I keep moving slowly and steadily towards my goals. Who knows - perhaps this is why I was chosen to endure an illness that persisted for a long period of time. I am the 'tortoise'; not the 'hare'. Persistence is my strength. And in the end, I persevered and crossed the finish line, just like the 'tortoise'.

At 40 years old, I felt like I was at the top of my game. My work as a nurse gave me great satisfaction. I had a wonderful family, two thriving teenage daughters and a loving husband. My days were very busy: work, church and organizational meetings, fitness workouts, visits with friends and relatives, and my daughters' sporting events. I had never been sick. In fact, my family doctor did not even know me.

When I discovered a lump on my breast, I was really not fazed. I *knew* that *I* was an unlikely candidate for breast cancer due to my healthy lifestyle and the fact that there was no history of the disease in my family. However, since I had just turned forty years-old, I scheduled my first routine mammogram. This mammogram would change my life forever and turn my world upside down. I was diagnosed with breast cancer and, unfortunately, it had spread extensively through my lymph nodes. I was given a 50/50 chance of living another five years. **A 50/50 chance....!** Never before had I realized that many women actually died from breast cancer. Living another five years was not enough for me. I wanted fifty-five more years. I had to beat this thing and be completely cured. Those 50/50 odds actually empowered me and drove me to fight harder.

Donna in remission, April 2004, with her family
L - R: husband Steve, daughter Lindsay, daughter Jessica and Donna

I elected to have surgery to remove the cancer and then faced the fight of my life. I bravely (maybe naively) vowed to defeat this disease and told myself that no cancer was going to keep me down. *'I am woman. I am strong.' I can do this!* As soon as I had recovered from the surgery, I started to prepare physically for the toughest game in which I would ever play. I went back to my exercise routine with even greater determination. I even added swimming to my workout to stretch and rebuild my arm muscles which had become weak and stiff as a result of the surgery.

Feeling stronger, I was now ready to begin the chemotherapy part of my treatment. As a nurse, I was fully aware that toxic chemicals would be pumped through my system, and this totally went against my principles to keep my body pure. I had always avoided taking even a Tylenol and, luckily, never needed much medication. I decided that I needed to get into a more optimistic healing frame of mind, so I began positive mental imagery and yoga. I read stories of survivors and began researching my disease and treatments extensively. I even imagined that the "chemo" were little Pac Men that would gobble up the bad cancerous cells as they encountered them.

The day of my first chemo, my daughters had their biggest softball game of the season. Since I felt guilty that I would miss the game, I made banners and posters to cheer the team on and filled a cooler full of drinks for the players. Watching my girls play their sports has always been my favorite pastime. Both girls always looked for my husband and me at their events and relaxed once they saw us. I felt awful that we would miss the game, but once I knew that my daughters were set for the day, I turned my thoughts toward what lay ahead.

My husband and I walked silently into the "chemo" clinic. I pretended to be brave, but was actually quite afraid of the unknown. Luckily, several members of my family arrived a few minutes later to help cheer me on. This definitely boosted my spirits, and in my "chemo bag", I was armed with an arsenal of religious statues, rosaries and books to keep me inspired.

I got through my first session with only a headache and left for home. My husband put me to bed. I had a vague feeling of nausea, and I presumptuously quipped, 'This isn't so bad. I can handle it.' But as I lay in bed, a vile sensation started to spread and grow in me. It filled my whole body. My head felt like it was about to explode, and soon I was wreathing in discomfort and bathed in sweat. Long waves of nausea overcame me, and I vomited. Wave after wave came, and my head was reeling. It was relentless. Nothing relieved it. It was by far the worst I have ever felt. In desperation, my family called my doctor who added another anti-nausea medication to my regimen. My discomfort continued, and they phoned my physician again, begging for help. Another combination of medications was prescribed, and I eventually drifted off into a drugged sleep...

The next eighteen months, I encountered one pitfall after

another and often felt as if I could hardly keep going. I read some-where that God brings some of the most exquisite 'flowers' through the dirt and dark, and I wondered when I would see the 'flowers' again. Many 'chemo' experiences and four surgeries later, I realized something very important. I had very little control over my destiny. I had always been the caregiver, the one in control, and this was a very humbling experience for me. God taught me this lesson over and over again. Each time I would think that I was on top of things and getting my life together, he would give me another challenge.

I have been cancer-free for two years now and am feeling like a much improved version of my old self. Through strict diet and exercise, I am back in shape again, and I feel strong – 'like a winner'. I don't know what tomorrow will bring, but who does? I love and appreciate each and every day and no longer 'sweat the small stuff'. My 'flowers' have finally bloomed at the finish line, and since I am the 'tortoise', I stop and smell them."

CHAPTER EIGHT
THIRD QUARTER –

CHARLIE'S STORY

If you are past half-time, you've moved on to the third quarter of life – ages 42 to 60. I can hardly believe that I am 43 years-old. Middle-aged! For some reason, though, I have never liked that term. It always seemed so.... *not young*! I think if it were referred to, instead, as the middle of growing (vs.aging), it would have a more positive connotation. Actually, I've always maintained that age is just a number - nothing more. Physical and mental condition are much more accurate measures of a person's well-being. We all know people who are a "young fifty" and others who are an "old twenty-eight". In truth, our real age and quarter of life is relative to our individual life span. For instance, if someone lives to be 100 years-old, then 30 years-old to 70 years-old would be middle age. Conversely, if a person should die at age 45, middle age would have been in his/her twenties! Because we just can't predict when the "end of the game" is for any of us, none of us knows when we are truly middle-aged. So for now, let's do away with defining middle age in terms of numbers. Instead, let's talk about what really matters in this quarter of life, what's really happening in our lives during this age period.

First of all, our bodies are visibly changing more significantly than in our second quarter. We're noticing more gray hair and more wrinkles. We're also noticing *less* hair on our heads and more hair on parts of our bodies that never had hair before! At this time in life, it is so much easier to gain extra weight and so much more difficult to get rid of it than it was ten years earlier. Just trying to *maintain* our weight becomes somewhat of a feat. In fact, even if we weigh the same as we did twenty years ago (if we're so lucky!), we just don't look the same as we did then.

This is the time we also begin to experience more stiffness and pain in our bones and joints. After a weekend of yard work or when it is cold and damp outside, you may just wake up wondering, "What am I going to be like when I'm older if I feel this stiff now?" Arthritis, bursitis, and other genetic problems tend to arise during this quarter, so when you study your genetic history - potential genetic problems – you should be on the lookout for heart disease, stroke, cancer, high blood pressure, and high levels of cholesterol. Risk factors begin to surface more at fifty-plus years than in any other age category and, therefore, you really need to understand where you've come from in order to understand where you may be headed.

This third quarter of life is, perhaps, *the* most critical quarter to make some significant personal play changes. For many people, how this quarter is handled can have a huge impact on the rest of their lives. Life choices are questioned. Are we doing the things we wanted to do in our lives? Do we have the career or job satisfaction we hoped for? Is our financial situation satisfactory? Are we physically and mentally strong enough to enjoy life for another twenty to thirty-plus years? Are we happy and satisfied with ourselves? Unfortunately for many, the answer is *no*. But we are about to get one last chance to change our game plan. Well, let's not say *last* chance, because I am a firm believer that it is never too late to make important changes; however, this big push for a possible game plan change is so important that, if you miss it, you could regret it for the rest of your life.

Now I know this time of life is full of ups and downs, and some of you are experiencing the "empty nest" effect with your kids now in college or off on their own. Yet, it gives you the perfect opportunity to concentrate on your own physical and mental fitness. You can do things that there was just no time to do when the kids were home. Some of you are in the perfect job environment and experiencing the rewards of many years of focused labor, while others are frustrated and unhappy, wondering if it's too late to make a career change at this age! Some people have been lucky enough to have had perfect health all these years and are firmly dedicated to a life of exercise and healthy eating habits, knowing that this is the best way to enjoy a high quality of life. A great number of people, though, have had no such luck in staying healthy. Of course, we cannot prevent every illness or injury by following a "game plan", but there is no doubt that we could enjoy a far better quality of life if we took care of ourselves. This is the time to take a good hard look at where we're headed. Our next quarter is when we retire. Our next quarter has the word *elderly* attached to it! Do what you have to do to put yourself in a winning frame of mind <u>now</u>. Whether it's your health, your career, your family situations, or you're just accomplishing something you've always wanted to do - but never got around to doing – don't waste this precious time! Don't procrastinate by thinking it's already too late, because that simply isn't true. As Nike says, "Just do it!**"**

And "Just do it!" is what my friend, Charlie, did.

CHARLIE'S STORY

One afternoon about ten or fifteen years ago, a gentleman with snow white hair and a white beard walked up to the front desk of my health club. Handsome, but a bit overweight, he looked to be in his mid to late-fifties. I could tell by his demeanor that he was not feeling good about himself. We shook hands, smiled at each other, and he began his story,

"Hello," he said, "I'm Charlie, and I need to join your health club."

"You *need* to join my health club? Well, I appreciate that!" I said, a bit puzzled by the fact that he *had* to join my club. "Charlie, why do you *need* to join?"

"Well," he replied, "My doctor just gave me my annual physical, and he wasn't pleased. My blood pressure is too high even

*Charlie Killinger (center) with his work out buddies
at PowerHouse Gym in Harrisburg, PA*

though I've been on medication for years, and I couldn't even complete a stress test. He said I may develop problems with my heart especially since I'm about fifty pounds overweight. I'm somewhat depressed, have absolutely no energy, and don't feel good about myself. To be honest with you, I'm a physical and nervous wreck."

"Wow!" I said, "I'm glad you're here, then. Tell me, Charlie, what do you do for a living? What kind of a lifestyle have you been living over the years?"

"Well, I'm a manager for an electric company," he said, "and I've been doing it for twenty-seven years. Usually I go to the American Legion after work for a couple of beers, and I hate to admit it, but while I'm there I snack on potato chips. I can't help it. I love those things! Then I go home and eat a big dinner with my wife. I might have another drink or two, watch a little television, enjoy a snack, and then go to bed. The next day I do just about the exact same thing!"

Twenty-seven years of the same routine, and as the old expression goes, *same old stuff, different day.* Many people get trapped in the *same old stuff, different day* routine, and as we age <u>we must</u> break that routine. Otherwise, it will control us and continue to negatively affect the quality of our lives. I firmly believe that we can be in control so that we can get the most out of the rest of our lives. With this in mind, I told Charlie, "I'll tell you what. I want to help you. I want to get you where you want to be, but you have to promise me one thing."

I'll never forget his reply. Charlie was sitting in my office in a chair right in front of my desk. "Hmmm," he said, what would that one thing be?" He sat forward, listening intently.

"You must commit to yourself," I replied, "not to me, not to your wife, not even to your doctor. You have to challenge yourself to do the right things to stay healthy, because if you don't, you might not be around for your next annual physical!"

Charlie leaned back and frowned. "You know what? That's exactly what my doctor told me. He said that if I don't change, I may not be around much longer. The only thing is I'm not even sure I *can* exercise! I've never really done it. I didn't even play any sports in high school!"

I stood up then, and Charlie followed me. As we walked out of the office and into the gym area, I turned to Charlie and told him, "You have a choice, and it's really pretty simple. You can *commit* to getting and staying fit … or not." Well – when I said that word *commit* again, you'd have thought I had asked Charlie to marry me! He actually began to shake nervously. "Look, Charlie," I said, "I can tell that you're unsettled about this whole thing, and I don't like to have people make these decisions under pressure. Why don't you go home and think about it. When you're ready, just come back in, and we'll get to work."

Well, the very next day, who should walk in but Charlie. He must have taken our conversation the day before seriously, because he was wearing a brand new sweat suit. I was surprised that he had made up his mind so quickly.

"I'm ready to join," he said enthusiastically, "and I want to join for a whole year, because if I don't, I may quit. I'm motivated! I have two beautiful granddaughters whom I want to see grow up!"

"That's smart, Charlie," I said. "That really does show your commitment…..at least financially, but a lot of people join health clubs with good intentions. They join for a year, and then they stop coming. For some reason, though, I do believe you're going to stick with this. From all the people I've trained throughout the years, I've learned one thing: some people stick with it, but most people don't.

You seem like the type of guy who will stick with it, though, because you have a specific reason for doing so... your granddaughters."

Charlie made the commitment that very day, and as time went on, it was amazing to see how much he transformed himself. When he started, he could barely bench press forty-five pounds. That's the weight of the bar alone. Needless to say, he was very weak and a little embarrassed as well.

I tried to encourage him. "I know you're looking at some of the other people here, and they're bigger and stronger. I don't want you to think for even a moment, though, that they're better than you and that you can't do this, because you can. We all had to start somewhere. You just have to walk before you run, so hang in there with it. Before you know it, you'll be seeing results."

So, Charlie hung in there, never giving up. When he turned sixty-one five years later, he could bench press 300 pounds - from 45 pounds to 300 pounds.... I could hardly believe it! Charlie had enormous inner strength and drive, but he never knew it until he faced serious health problems and was confronted with a choice in life: take control and make your best effort to win, or take your chances and expect to lose. Charlie began feeling good about himself mentally, spiritually, and emotionally. Physically, he looked fantastic! His body fat percentage dropped down to 19%, which is fabulous for a man his age. His strength was incredible, and he eventually went off of his blood pressure medication and got his cholesterol under control. His weight was normal for his height. He felt like a new man – absolutely restored. He went through this restoration process like a classic antique car that's been around for a while – one that's been used and abused, but now put back into showroom condition. In fact, Charlie felt *so* good about himself, one day I caught him flexing in front of the mirrors at the club.

"Charlie," I said, "you look fantastic, but I think this is starting to go to your head!"

"Mark," he replied, "I want to be a model. I've always wanted to be a model."

"Really???" I answered in disbelief.

"Yeah, I feel so good, I want to get in front of people and show them just how good I feel!" he said, flashing a smile.

I said, "Charlie, you're amazing! I know of a modeling agency here in town. Let me give you their number, and you can give them a call. Tell them I sent you."

I gave him the number before he left the gym that day, but I never really expected him to make the phone call, and I never heard another word about it from Charlie. What a surprise it was when browsing through the "Lifestyle" section of the Sunday Patriot News a few months later, I came upon.... Charlie! Sure enough, there he was in a big ad for cataract surgery. Maybe not the most glamorous thing to model for, but he had actually made it, and that was just the beginning. Soon he began doing runway work, fashion shows, and more print jobs.

It just goes to show that it's never too late to make positive changes. Here was Charlie, well into his third quarter, and he completely turned his physical condition around. Now when he retired, not only could he enjoy his granddaughters, but also his improved quality of life. He made the commitment and stuck with it. So many people wait until it's too late, or almost too late. Keep in mind, there are many, many changes that we need to make as we age. It's not simply getting more physically fit. We need to become more emotionally and spiritually fit as well. It's a total package, and it's very difficult to do, but it's something that *needs* to be done.

I tell this story about Charlie because so many people believe that they're too old to make changes and see positive results but, of course, it's really never too late. Just regroup, put your game face on, and work on making the play changes necessary to win that game whether they are better eating habits, adding or increasing an exercise program, changing your thought process, or simply working on your personal attitude. We all need to better ourselves somehow. It's so easy to become complacent and so difficult to change. As human beings, by nature, we want to make ourselves comfortable. Unfortunately, being *comfortable* often means being complacent, and being complacent just doesn't get you ahead in the game. Remember – the game isn't over yet. <u>It's time to hustle!</u>

CHAPTER NINE
FOURTH QUARTER

VICTORY IN THE MAKING

Let's look at that fourth quarter, 62 to 80 years of age ... the "golden years" as they say. These are the seasoned players, the ones with the most wisdom, the players with that valuable knowledge that many of us have not yet acquired.

During the fourth quarter, we begin to view life a bit differently. Just as we talked about school and parties during our First Quarter, and children and careers during our Second and Third Quarters, we talk about different things in our Fourth Quarter. Let's envision ourselves in our late seventies or early eighties gathered together at a social function. What do you think our topic of conversation will include? When I ask that question in a training seminar, it's interesting to listen to people's responses. Most attendees are in the Second and Third Quarters of life; a few in the First and Fourth. They say that those in the Fourth Quarter talk mostly about the good old days, their families, grandkids, and their aches and pains. Those are the topics that many would have in common at that age. However, another very typical conversation might be about who recently passed away. When seasoned players pick up the newspaper, where do you think they most often turn first? You guessed it, the obituaries. They're interested in who **left the game of life** most

Mark's grandfather, Salvatore Busa

recently. Think about it. If you're 32, you chat to your friends about who just had a baby, but when you're 78.....

   My wife's grandmother will attest to that. She is a feisty 94 year-old lady still living on her own in a high-rise community in Hershey, PA. She has a great attitude and keeps herself active. She participates in most of the social events in her building, so she knows almost everyone else who lives there. They play cards or bingo a couple of times a week, chatting and enjoying each other's company.

My wife's grandmother Luella Brown, age 94
with my son Marcus

She has often told us of the neighbor who was carried off to the hospital the night before, or about this friend or that friend who is now in a nursing home or has recently passed away.

When you're in the First Quarter of Life, it's virtually impossible to comprehend the Fourth Quarter. Even when you enter the Second Quarter of life and you're approaching half-time, it's still pretty tough to imagine yourself at 80 years old. I'm in my Third Quarter, and it *still* seems a long way off! Because of this, we may *think* about our retirement plans but, for the most part, we cannot even fathom actually *using* them. We know, though, that planning for the future is the wise thing to do, and we begin to do it. As we enter into the Third Quarter, however, retirement begins to take on a bit more importance than it did before, but it's primarily from a financial viewpoint. It still seems far away, but before you know it, you're actually IN the Fourth Quarter – a senior, one of life's seasoned players! Where did all the years go? That passage of time, constantly moving forward as we go about our daily business, seems to quicken its pace as we grow older. I've spoken with numerous seasoned players during my travels, and when I asked if their years had passed by slowly or quickly, each one's answer was always the same. "I can't believe that 80 years have actually gone by!" Yes, the clock is ticking for all of us, but as you enter the Fourth Quarter of life, the time left on the clock becomes even more precious.

My grandfather, Salvatore, had a tremendous influence on me, and he taught me his philosophy on the Fourth Quarter. He lived to 90 years of age, beating the national statistics of the average males' life span, 76-80 years-old. Although, technically an overtime player in life, my grandfather loved his Fourth Quarter. Having lived through very tough times as a child and young adult, he appreciated every moment of his Fourth Quarter right up to the end of his life.

I'll never forget the night he died. We were celebrating at our annual Christmas party in my home with friends, family members and business associates when my mother called me. She was sobbing and said the hospital had called to tell her that they didn't think my grandfather would make it through the night. I rushed out of the party with one of my best friends so I could share the last few moments of my Grandfather's life. The rest of my family left the party as well, and we gathered together in his hospital room. The emotions were incomprehensible, but seeing my grandfather so peaceful and happy, comforted all of us. He was truly ready to finish out his game of life. He was able to make contact with us all, gasping for breath as we said our farewells to him. It was an awesome experience; my grandfather was victorious to the end, and after he died, we all went back to the party to celebrate my Grandfather's life.

I've interviewed many seniors and have found their viewpoints quite compelling. They tend to appreciate their time and do not take things for granted. I've heard many say that their stress levels are not as high as when they were younger. Why? Their kids are grown, they are no longer working, and they've put their lives into perspective. There are other seasoned players, though, that have informed me that they have high levels of stress. This is often due to finances or health-related issues. Their health problems, in many cases, stem from neglecting to manage their lifestyle factors - sleep, stress, nutrition, mental and physical exercise, and attitude.

This is also when most people retire, but unfortunately, many who retire from work, also retire from life. On the other hand, there are those who really begin to *live*. They enjoy life to its fullest: traveling, golfing, fishing, and doing things that they never had time for before. Let's face facts! If you've taken good care of yourself while you were younger and continue to do so into your later years, your quality of life is typically better, and the risk of health problems is reduced when you start to manage yourself, even in the Fourth Quarter. This is easier said than done, though. We know this. We've developed habits that are not easy to break, and looking back, you might think that there are many things you would have done differently; however, dwelling on the past is not productive in executing your game plan to age now. Instead, move forward. Start today to regain some momentum by managing your lifestyle factors. Something as simple as walking three days per week, or stretching daily, will make you feel better. Eat healthier foods on a regular basis, and maintain a positive attitude. This is your wake up call; one that isn't too late. Gain a new outlook on life. You'll have more energy, and daily living will become more enjoyable. Even the simple things, such as getting out of bed in the morning or working in the garden, will seem easier. Make each and every day count. If you're not yet in the Fourth Quarter, don't wait! Make it easier on yourself later on by managing your lifestyle factors *now*. But if you *are* in the Fourth Quarter, take the ultimate challenge. Make life a victory!

BEN CAIN'S STORY

I'd like to share with you an inspiring story of a gentleman I met through the Department of Aging. His name was Ben Cain. It was late October many years ago, when I first received a call from Ben.

"Hi, my name is Ben Cain, and I want to work for you," he said with a *lot* of exuberance.

"Hello," I answered, "Excuse me?"

"Yes," he repeated, "I'm Ben Cain, and I want to be in the health and fitness business."

"What kind of experience do you have, Ben?" I asked.

"Well," he replied, "I don't have much experience in it at all, but I know it's a business I'd like to be in!"

"Fine," I said, interested to meet him, "Why don't we set up an interview?"

"That will be fantastic," said Ben, "I'll be in to see you tomorrow. I was intrigued by his aggressiveness, and I could tell just by talking to him over the phone that I was talking to an enthusiastic older gentlemen, but I couldn't tell how old.

So the next day at ten o'clock in the morning, Ben Cain rushed through the door, all dressed up in a suit.

"Hello! I'm Ben Cain!"

"Nice to meet you, Ben. How are you doing?"

He was enthusiastic, in his late 70's or early 80's, and wanted very much to be in the health and fitness business. "Ben," I said, "What's motivating you? You seem to have more energy than a lot of folks in their twenties!"

Ben Kain

"Well," he said, "I'm a former Dale Carnegie instructor, and I had my own sales and motivational company for many years. I was lacking one thing though. I always had the mental part of life covered, but I did nothing with the physical part. I never really took good care of myself. In fact, not too long ago, I was backing out of my driveway with my wife next to me and I couldn't even turn my head to look in the rear window to get out of the driveway. I remember complaining to my wife, 'Honey, I can't turn my head to look out the rear window; what's the matter with me?' My wife just teased me, telling me I was an old man! And you know what? I'd never really thought about it before, but it hit me like a flash! I AM old! I never thought of myself as an old man until that day, and that's when I decided I had to do something about it. I couldn't allow myself to just *be old*!

So I decided to enroll in a health club, and I began to exercise. I started to feel body parts and muscles that I'd never felt in my entire life. My range of motion improved. I even had more energy. In fact, I felt so vibrant, it was as if I'd been recharged for the balance of my life. I never did any real physical exercise until now, and I'm in my late 70's, so I'm a firm believer that this is one of the areas that could lead to the Fountain of Youth, and I want to be involved!"

Well, following that interview with Ben, I knew I wanted to work with him. I felt he could be a great asset to inspire other people, and through my involvement with the Department of Aging, I saw a perfect fit.

I phoned him and said, "Ben, I think I have a job for you. I want you to help me motivate senior citizens to take better care of themselves. You're in the same age group, and I think that would be very motivating for them!" "Mark," he said, "I'd love to team up with you and help. A lot of people think they're too old and so far gone that they can't make a change. I'd *love* to help them get well for the balance of time they have here. I am at your service."

So Ben began working with me. He became a motivational speaker for the senior community centers and assisted living homes. The impact that he made was tremendous! He developed an exercise program and a positive attitude system for senior citizens to become more active as they aged and called it *The Stay Younger Club*. He got people motivated and moving. He helped people in their 70's and 80's to make very exciting changes for themselves. In 2003, Ben and his wife, Grace, were awarded the honor of Capital Blue Cross's Senior Healthy Heroes for Central Pennsylvania, a well deserved recognition to them both.

Sadly, though, Ben passed away this past year at the age of 89. He was a true inspiration; a gentleman who changed his ways, enhancing his and other's overall quality of life, well into the Fourth Quarter. Ben turned the game around at the last minute. He was a winner.

An Important Note

There are those who have been diagnosed with serious health problems and have not taken the advice of their physicians or changed their behaviors. For many, their lives were cut short. When people are diagnosed with health problems, fear can take over. Some channel that fear in a positive direction and make the necessary changes. But others allow that fear to take control of their lives. They don't channel the fear, or redirect it, to positive actions that are necessary to overcome this type of challenge.

There is an old saying: '*We spend our entire lives sacrificing our health to gain money. Then when we get to retirement we spend all of our money to try and regain our health*'. How true it is! BUT DO YOU WANT THAT TO BE YOU?

Remember my best friend Ed? He said, *"Try until you die!"* If <u>YOU</u> do, your Fourth Quarter will be the Victory Quarter in the game of life.

My "Pap", Salvatore Busa.

PART III

YOUR PERSONAL

GAMEPLAN

PERFORMANCE NUTRITION: EATING FOR ENERGY TO AGE

BACK TO BASICS

We hear so much about nutrition: diet, eating, disorders, nutrition related diseases, obesity, words that scare us and make us think we must change our eating habits. But changing behavior is a complex process. Most of us have probably been eating the same way since our youth. If you think about the foods that you ate as a child, I bet most of you still crave them. They have become a habit to you.

A couple of years ago a police officer approached me after a training that I was giving for the police force. He said that he needed to lose 100 pounds quickly. He asked if I would help him figure out a diet, because the police force informed him that he would lose his job if he didn't take off a considerable amount of weight. We walked out to his car and talked about his health problems.

He said, "Mark, I have this incredible craving for mayonnaise, and I need to eat it every day." I didn't think much of that comment until he opened his trunk and pointed to a box that contained several large jars of mayonnaise.

"Why do you carry around a case of mayonnaise?" I asked.

"Because I eat one large jar a day," he replied.

"Why?" I asked, obviously stunned at the amount of mayonnaise he was consuming.

"Because as I grew up, my mother put mayonnaise on everything. I guess I got used to the taste. I can't seem to get away from it."

It's so true that habits are hard to break, even good ones. If your mom made healthy foods, more than likely, you are making healthy food choices too. But chances are your parents were *not* health conscious. Only in the past fifteen years have people begun to realize how important our food intake is to our overall health. Everyday there is information that relates nutrition to health, so we all know we must change our eating habits. But how do we do it? Before we begin to change our habits, we must know what to do. I have a plan that I guarantee can change your eating habits. It's easy to follow, and it will give you positive results. I call it "THE WHY, WHERE, WHEN, WHAT AND HOW OF NUTRITION."

THE BASIC NUTRITION EATING PLAN

- Eat vegetables in abundance and fruits one to three times a day.
- Eat whole grains at most meals; limit white rice, white bread, potatoes and pasta.
- Reduce saturated fat and cholesterol; limit red meats and butter.
- Drink water.
- Eat healthy snacks; limit sweets and salt

THE WHY...

We seem to overlook the reasons *why* we eat. We need to understand our emotions toward food before we can begin to make changes in our eating habits. Emotions affect why and what we eat. Eating can be pure enjoyment for some; for others it can be a source of diversion or frustration. We eat certain foods out of habit, or we associate certain foods with different times in our lives.

My friend, Susan, has three children, Steve, Dan, and

Madelyn. When the kids were growing up, Susan used to cut fresh fruit into small pieces as a treat for them when they walked into the house after school. It became a ritual. On days that she didn't feeling like cutting fruit, Dan would nag and whine, "Mom, please cut me fruit." Out of guilt, she would comply. Dan went off to Johns Hopkins University years later and one day sent Susan a paper he had written for his creative writing class. It was called, "My Mom Cuts Me Fruit." The entire paper told how Dan's mom cut him fruit every day after school and how he still associates fruit with love. Anytime he sees fruit cut up in small pieces, a warm feeling goes through him. Susan read the paper and sighed. "Oh, how I wish I had known that back then. I wouldn't have complained about cutting him fruit!"

We eat certain foods at certain times of the year. Think about how much more food most of us eat during the holiday season. Sure, it's because we are surrounded by lots of tasty choices, but the emotion of the holiday comes into play as well. We may eat more because we are lonely during the holidays, or we may not eat certain foods because we won't fit into that outfit we want to wear.

We often eat, or don't eat, because we want to look a certain way. Does this conversation sound familiar to you? It occurred between two of my colleagues. Sally was on another one of her diets. They were at the office, and Rob walked out of the conference room with two donuts. Rob smiled and offered one to Sally.

Sally: "No thanks. I'd love to eat that, but it's not part of my diet.
Rob: "Which diet are you on now?"
Sally: "Oh, it's the latest. Best findings yet. Remember the last one I was on? Well they found out it just doesn't work. I felt irritable and angry a lot of the time."
Rob: "I remember you being on that diet. You thought it was the answer for you."
Sally: "Yes, for awhile I did, but I was wrong. This one seems to make me feel happy, and I am getting good results. Can you tell? I lost six pounds."
Rob: "You really do look good, Sally, but why don't you just eat what you want and enjoy life?"

Sally: "The reasons are endless, Rob. I hate the way I look, and I have low energy. By the time I walk into the house at night, I can't even play with the kids, I'm so beat. I'm moody a lot of the time, and I was just diagnosed with diabetes."

Rob: "Wow! So this latest diet...do you really think it's the right one? It seems like it's been a guessing game for you!"

How often does that occur? Diet in...diet out. Diets just don't seem to be working. Obesity is at epidemic proportions; high blood pressure is on the rise, and almost every other person I know has either some sort of heart problem or diabetes. Why is this happening? We should be the healthiest of nations; yet we are not. How much stems from our lifestyle and, in particular, our diet?

We need to start looking at our diet in a different way. Food is more than a packaged dinner off the shelf at the supermarket or a diet that has been advertised as the ultimate way to lose weight. Food is our source of energy, and we can't live without it. It is also a source of habit to us; however, and unless we know how to change this habit of eating the wrong foods, we will continue to go from one diet to another...just like Sally.

Think about what makes *you* eat the way you do. Be honest. Are you the kind of person who eats only traditional foods; those you grew up with or are a part of your religion? Or do you eat because of the advertisements you watch on TV? Perhaps you eat out of social pressure or boredom? When you don't have anything else to do, do you grab the chips? Most of us have many reasons why we eat. Think about the reasons you eat.

WHY I EAT THE WAY I DO...

1. I choose foods based on my mood of the day.	Yes _____	No _____
2. I often eat even though I am full.	Yes _____	No _____
3. I eat when I am anxious, frustrated, or depressed.	Yes _____	No _____
4. I eat certain foods out of habit.	Yes _____	No _____
5. When I am in a hurry, I often grab unhealthy foods.	Yes _____	No _____
6. I eat because of advertisements I see on TV.	Yes _____	No _____
7. I eat when I am lonely or stressed.	Yes _____	No _____
8. I have been on more than one diet in the past 2 years.	Yes _____	No _____
9. I feel that food controls my life.	Yes _____	No _____
10. I am not happy with my body.	Yes _____	No _____
11. I eat because nutrition is important to my well-being.	Yes _____	No _____
12. I eat to socialize with those people important to me.	Yes _____	No _____
13. I eat because food tastes good to me.	Yes _____	No _____
14. I eat healthy foods to prevent disease and stay healthy.	Yes _____	No _____

If your answer was yes to questions 1-10, think about the reasons why you eat the way you do. What does food mean to you? Why do you crave the foods you do? How do you feel about yourself when you eat foods that you don't think are good for you? Do you carry around a lot of negative thoughts concerning food?

You may have several reasons why you want to change your eating habits. Maybe you've gained weight over the years. Maybe you're afraid of the health hazards related to the foods you are eating. Maybe you have been involved in a difficult relationship and you turned to food for comfort. Whatever your reason may be, it is important for you to think about why you eat the way you do.

At a party, over soufflé spinach balls, a friend cornered me with his plan to lose weight. He had what he thought was a terrific idea for a diet and asked me my opinion. Although he had never really been eating properly, he thought he would start by cutting out all of those foods that caused him heartburn.

"Fine," I said. "Then when you get frustrated with a situation at work, what foods will you eat?"

"Why are you asking me that?" he questioned, looking puzzled.

"Because you can't just say that you will cut out foods that cause you heartburn. Those foods may be the ones that are part of your tradition. If you were raised on them, you may find you have a problem just eliminating them."

Jim, another friend, joined in the conversation. "So what does that mean, Mark?"

"It means that awareness of why you eat certain foods is your first step in losing weight, or in choosing healthy foods. Think about why you eat the foods you do. Most people have been taught to eat certain foods when they were young, and then those food habits become a part of who they are. You have to look at what food means to you, what things influence your food choices, and why you eat.

"I eat for different reasons," Jim said, "But after I have those chicken wings, I feel guilty. I feel like I'm a bad person, and it really drives me nuts, but I don't stop eating the wings!"

"Jim," I said, "You have to stop judging yourself. You're the best you can be right now. That doesn't mean that you can't change, but stop judging yourself based on your diet. Separate yourself from your behavior. Just because you eat a certain way doesn't mean that you *always* have to eat that way. It's only the behavior that has to change...not who you are, and you have to have a reason to *want* to change."

Think about your eating habits and jot down some thoughts you have concerning your relationship to food.

I eat the way I do because

_____

_____

_____

_____

I want to change my eating habits because

_____

_____

_____

_____

If I don't change my eating habits I may

_____

_____

_____

_____

You have to have a reason, and it has to be something very important to you if you really want to change your eating habits. This brings to mind a situation that happened to my cousin, Joan. Joan was in great health about twenty years ago. She was in her thirties, and she didn't think about what she ate. She was thin, in great physical shape, and the guys always turned and looked at her. I remember asking her how she stayed looking so good, because I would see all the high fat foods she ate. She said that it didn't matter what she ate. "I can eat anything. I guess I'm just lucky." Joan was in the Second Quarter of life, so she didn't show signs of ill health, which isn't unusual. She continued eating whatever looked yummy at the moment. She didn't think about whether the food was good for her. It just didn't matter. Year after year, I'd see her at family reunions still eating those high fat, high sugar foods.

She moved to the west coast and I didn't see her for a number of years. Then last year she came to a cousins' reunion. I hardly recognized her. She had gained weight, her complexion was poor, and she looked like she could barely walk to the buffet table.

"Hey, Mark," Joan said.

"Is that you, Joan?" I replied.

"I guess I look different than I did the last time you saw me. My kids are now six, eight and eleven, and that hasn't helped my figure. My life is really messed up."

"Why?" I asked.

"Well, I should have known that our family's health history would catch up with me since my dad died of a heart attack at such a young age. My mom has diabetes and high blood pressure. And you know Aunt Bess was diagnosed with breast cancer. I'm doomed. What are my chances of good health? I gained weight over the years, got my mom's high blood pressure, and just got a report from the doctor that I need a triple by pass."

"Joan" I said, "I'm your cousin, and I don't feel doomed. What have you done for yourself as far as your health?"

"What do you mean? What can I do? I am doomed. How can you say I'm not?" she asked.

"I don't think you are. I think that lots of people are starting to realize that the kinds of foods we put into our bodies are very important. Physicians, dentists, scientists, teachers, and yes, moms like you are all realizing that there is a big need for all of us to eat foods that will help us stay healthy. There are so many nutrition related diseases in our society today."

"It's just too late for me," she moaned.

"No, I don't believe it is. Sure it would have helped if you had eaten healthier foods twenty years ago, but it isn't too late to start taking care of yourself now. Every disease that you named is affected by nutrition. Most people have someone who has a nutrition related disease in their family."

"What are these nutrition related diseases?" Joan asked.

"Nutrition related diseases are diseases that have some connection to nutrition; that is, diseases like obesity or heart disease are either partially or completely caused by nutritional habits, or diseases like diabetes and cancer must be controlled by nutritional habits. If someone in the family has one or more of these nutrition related diseases, you run the risk of getting it yourself. But you can also lessen that risk."

"I guess there's nothing I can do about it now," Joan said negatively.

"You CAN do something about it. I bet your doctor has advised you to cut back on fat."

"You're right, and I have, but what can I do about my health now?"

"Joan," I said, "If you have a car that you love, you probably take good care of it so it will last a long time. True?"

"Well, I just got a new white Camry SE, and I'm taking great care of it," Joan said.

"Think about this," I replied. "If you don't get your Camry checked out, or if you don't take good care of it, it's not the end of the world. With money, you can go and buy a new car. But you can't walk into a body shop and buy a new body. You have one body for the rest of your life, and you can't replace it if you don't take care of it. Your body and your health are the most valuable possessions you own."

"You are so right. I thought that I was healthy and that I would always stay healthy. I didn't consider all of the people in our family that had some kind of nutrition related disease."

"You know, Joan, you have a choice," I said. "The quality of your life can improve through proper nutrition."

I met with Joan several times and told her my plan. She sent me an email and, believe it or not, her high blood pressure is now under control. She still has to have the triple by pass surgery, but she is more optimistic about her future. She has taken control of her eating habits and even lost fifteen pounds.

She wrote, "Mark, once you told me about the nutrition related diseases in our family, and that I can prevent and be proactive rather than be passive, something clicked inside of me. I had a reason to change. I realized that I could take control of my own health and don't have to die young like my father did. My reason became that I want to be around to see my grandchildren, and at the rate I was going, there was no chance of that. But what I discovered is that my benefits aren't in the future. They're now. I wake up in the morning, and I am full of energy. I never realized how the food I was eating affected me during the day. I was grumpy and moody, but now my temperament is much more balanced. I even think I am going to start an exercise program." Nice ending. I know that Joan can't make up for those lost years, but the quality of her life is improving, and as you can see, she certainly feels a lot better.

Now that you know why you eat the way you do, and you have created a reason why you want to change, you have to know what to eat. You need the information. So here goes!

THE WHAT...

I don't want to complicate your life. Knowledge, simplicity, and convenience are the main objectives when I think of healthy food habits. You need to have the knowledge of what your body needs. Once you know what foods you need, and I don't mean rocket science knowledge, then you can choose those foods that you like and that your body needs. You also need to focus on simplicity. Your everyday diet should not be complicated. It should be simple to follow. Finally, it has to be convenient for you. It has to fit into your own particular needs; all of your emotional needs and also your everyday life. If I told you to change everything, you just wouldn't do it. You have to make it fit into your traditions and your daily lifestyle. Sure, you may have to make some lifestyle and behavioral changes, but these changes should be small. I like to say that small changes make for big gains.

So first, the basic knowledge: Nutrition is the science of how our bodies utilize the food we eat. Our bodies need more than 40 different nutrients for good health. Essential nutrients include vitamins, minerals, amino acids from protein, certain fatty acids from fat, and sources of calories from protein, carbohydrates and fat.

Optimum health cannot be attained without a well-balanced diet that is rich in all of the known nutrients. No single food item supplies all the essential nutrients in the amounts that you need. Milk, for instance, contains very little Vitamin C. Meat doesn't give you the carbohydrates your body needs. We need to eat a variety of foods to assure an adequate diet.

What we eat determines a good part of our health. Nutritional deficiency is one of the major problems in our society despite adequate food supply. The list of diseases that are affected by a lack of nutrients is long and overwhelming. From allergies to angina, from colitis to leg cramps...food affects how we feel and even how long we live.

Our bodies are made up of at least 57% water, 20% protein, 15% fat and 8% carbohydrates, minerals and vitamins. Proper nutrition means that all of these nutrients are in balance. Only when we replenish these nutrients constantly can we have good nutrition, which is essential for normal growth and maintenance for resistance to disease and for the ability to repair injuries.

We need to eat foods that supply our bodies with energy. Carbohydrates, fats, and protein are the three nutrients that supply fuel which gives our body heat and energy to live. Carbohydrates give us the most energy. They serve as the primary source of energy for all of our body functions and muscular action. Fats give us energy as well, but they also help make calcium available to body tissues, particularly to the bones and teeth. Protein is the building material for muscles, skin, hair, blood, nails and internal organs. Vitamins help to regulate our metabolism and convert fat and carbohydrates into energy. Minerals are important to regulate the skeletal structure and help to keep the heart and brain in good condition. They are also important in the production of hormones. So we need them all, and they are in a variety of foods.

EAT VEGETABLES AND FRUIT

VEGETABLES...AS MUCH AS YOU WANT! Vegetables provide us with all sorts of vitamins that our bodies need. If you eat a vegetable that is yellow or orange, it most likely has Vitamin A in it. There are also vegetables with a lot of Vitamin C, like brussel sprouts, green peppers and cabbage. There are vegetables that contain both Vitamin A and C. Dark green leafy vegetables have both. Vegetables give us fiber. Fiber helps move food through our intestinal tract more quickly so it doesn't sit there for too long. We need fiber to stimulate the digestive system, prevent constipation, and reduce the risk of digestive disorders. Fiber helps reduce the absorption of fat and helps slow the absorption of sugar.

Vegetables also have characteristics similar to our bodies. For instance, have you ever noticed when you look at a sliced carrot, you can actually see that it looks like an eye. Vitamin A in carrots, sweet potatoes, and squash promotes eye sight. Carrots are a rich source of beta carotene, which the body converts to vitamin A. Vitamin A helps prevent night blindness, cataracts and may have a role in preventing macular degeneration. Tomatoes are high in antioxidants, which help rid the body of free radicals, or harmful substances. Look at a tomato. It has the same shape as the chamber of your heart. Some initial studies are showing that people who eat an abundance of tomatoes have about half the risk of heart attack as those who don't eat any. Broccoli is another favorite of mine. Can you see that broccoli looks like the tubes to our stomach and to other organs in our bodies? When I look at broccoli, I see a resemblance to our own bodies. Even those tiny tree like parts in the broccoli look like the branches in our kidneys. I believe broccoli may be one of the most important vegetables to eat.

There are many ways to get the most nutrition from vegetables: Eat them raw. Cook them in water, but avoid soaking or cutting vegetables into small pieces, and use only a small amount of cooking water since some of the vitamins will be lost in the water. Steam vegetables. With steaming, the nutrients aren't lost in the water. Stir fry them using only a small amount of fat. Instead of high calorie sauces, season with pepper and herbs. Use dill with snap beans, oregano with eggplant, and basil with tomatoes. Or try a squeeze of lemon juice on green beans or carrots.

FRUITS...ONE TO THREE SERVINGS A DAY.

Fruit—a sign of nature. Nature is sending us signals. Fruits give us vitamins, minerals, fiber, and energy. Those fruits that fall from the tree in autumn are important for our bodies. The grapes in the vincyards are giving us a message. Even the looks of the fruits...again, I liken it to our bodies. Look at a banana. Doesn't it look strong and firm? Believe it or not, it is good for the muscles. Bananas are high in potassium, which studies show, improve circulation. Improved circulation helps our bodies get the blood to our muscles during exercise. Oranges have Vitamin C. Don't discount the skin of the orange, which looks like our skin in some ways. Citrus peels may help to prevent cancer. Red grapes play a role in increasing good cholesterol. Another resemblance. Look at a bunch of red grapes. Do you see the resemblance to the shape of your heart? Is it any wonder that we hear that red grapes increase good cholesterol? Eat at least one to three servings of fruit a day. A small apple, a banana, a pear are all servings of fruit.

EAT WHOLE GRAINS AT MOST MEALS

Your body requires breads, cereals, rice and pasta on a daily basis, but they should be whole grains and not the refined products that are so heavily advertised. You can eat as many as six to eleven servings of whole grains a day. You won't gain weight if you limit the refined products and many of the processed foods that are so readily available wherever we go, and instead, choose to eat whole grain products.

A whole grain is made up of three parts: the outermost layers of bran, the germ, and the largest portion called the endosperm. During refining, the coarse bran layers are removed to ease cooking and to provide the product with the desired white color. The germ is also removed because it contains oil, which shortens shelf life. The refined product is mainly composed of endosperm, yet it is the germ that provides much of the protein, vitamins and minerals. The bran serves as fiber. Enrichment of refined grains replaces only a few of the many nutrients and none of the fiber lost during processing.

Fiber is made up of a number of complex substances, which are all types of carbohydrates. They are only found in plants and come mainly from the plant cell walls. They fall into two groups: soluble fiber and insoluble fiber. Insoluble fiber is found mainly in wheat products like flour, bread, breakfast cereals, and bran. It is important because it acts rather like a sponge when we eat it, soaking up moisture in the stomach and swelling up. This makes us feel full and stimulates the digestive system. Soluble fiber is in fruits, vegetables, and legumes. Some of the richest sources of soluble fiber are red kidney beans, baked beans, dried peas, lentils, oats, barley and rye.

When you start the morning with whole-wheat bread and a bowl of whole-grain cereal like oatmeal or granola, you give yourself energy that will last throughout the day. Dark and whole-grain breads are an absolute in any healthy diet. The WHITES, as in white bread, white flour, white pasta won't do it!

You may say that you just don't like brown bread or whole wheat pasta, but it just may be that you aren't used to it. Whole wheat has a different taste than white flour, but I guarantee that if you give it a try for a few weeks, you will become accustomed to the taste, and you may well prefer it.

REDUCE SATURATED FAT AND CHOLESTEROL AND INCREASE THE GOOD FATS

There is so much to say about fats, yet sometimes it seems so confusing. The government says that you should limit your fat calories to no more than 30% of your total calories for the day. Only 10% of your fat calories should come from saturated fats and no more than

300 mg should be from foods high in cholesterol. Limit trans fatty Acids. But what does it all mean?

First of all, you need *some* fat every day. It is an important dietary component and provides us with fatty acids essential for growth and calories for body energy. It aids in the feeling of "fullness" and transports certain vitamins to different parts of the body. Fat acts as a carrier for fat-soluble vitamins A, D, E, and K. Fats give us different taste in foods, different textures, and it does taste good! But too much fat... and too much of the wrong kinds of fat, is a problem. It can lead to weight gain, obesity and heart disease.

Research has shown that there are definitely certain fats that we should eat; others that we should either drastically reduce or eliminate. The fats found in fatty fish like salmon, sardines, anchovies, albacore tuna, and mackerel have what's called omega-3 fatty acid, which are also found in walnuts, soybeans and flaxseeds. This fat helps the body to absorb bone-building calcium and is good for the heart. It makes the blood less likely to clot. A word about poultry, fish and legumes. When you eat white meat chicken or turkey breast and fish, you are getting protein and good sources of B vitamins, iron and zinc, which are also lower in cholesterol, fat, and calories than some types of meat. Legumes, such as soybeans, black beans, split peas, and lentils are good substitutes for meat because they give you protein and fiber without the cholesterol, fat or calories.

Then there are the unsaturated fats, which are also good for us because they do not raise our blood cholesterol. They occur in vegetable oils, most nuts, olives, avocados, and fatty fish like salmon.

Monounsaturated fat is an important fat, which is liquid at room temperature. It gets thicker when chilled. Olive, peanut, and canola oils are a good source of monounsaturated fat. They do not raise cholesterol. We should include this fat, or oil, into our daily diet. One of the best means of doing this is to use olive oil on our bread and eliminate the butter. We'd be doing our body a big favor.

It's the saturated fats that tend to raise blood cholesterol. Those are the ones that we have to reduce or even eliminate. They are solid at room temperature and get harder when chilled. They include: high-fat dairy products (like cheese, whole milk, cream, butter, and regular ice cream), processed meats, the skin and fat of poultry, and lard, palm oil, and coconut oil. No more than 10% of your daily fats should be saturated.

Another term that has popped into our vocabulary is called trans fatty acids. Foods that have trans fatty acids in them tend to raise blood cholesterol. They include: foods high in partially hydrogenated vegetable oils such as hard margarines and shortenings, and foods made through a process of hydrogenation that solidifies liquid oils. This process is put into foods to increase their shelf life and flavor. Some of these foods include: crackers, cookies, french fries, doughnuts, commercially fried foods and packaged snack foods. Beef, pork, and lamb also have natural trans fatty acids in them.

Now let's talk about cholesterol, a word used often when someone mentions diet. Cholesterol is a waxy, fat-like substance found in every animal cell, which is manufactured by the liver. It is present in all foods of animal origin. Our bodies need cholesterol because our nerve cells send messages back and forth with the aid of cholesterol. It helps our gallbladder make bile acids, which allows us to absorb fat and vitamins. It protects our cell membranes. But too much cholesterol in the diet can cause a buildup of a fatty substance in the arteries. Over a period of time these deposits clog the arteries and reduce the blood flow to the heart or brain. The result may be a heart attack or a stroke.

Foods high in cholesterol tend to raise blood cholesterol, so you should consume no more than 300 mg. of cholesterol a day. Cholesterol in food comes from animal sources, particularly organ meats such as brains, kidney and liver, egg yolk, fatty meats, shrimp, butter, lard, cream, whole milk and whole milk cheeses. There is no cholesterol found in plants. The label shows the amount of cholesterol in the food. For a food to be cholesterol free it must have less than 2 milligrams of cholesterol per serving and 2 grams or less of saturated fat per serving.

DRINK WATER

Water comprises approximately 83% of our blood, 73% of muscle tissue, 25% of body fat, and 22% of bone. Our bodies contain 10 to 12 gallons of water- up to 75% of our total body weight. Muscle holds more water than body fat, so the leaner you are, the more water your body contains.

We need to continually replace the water we lose. We can actually lose 80 to 90 ounces of water per day, and drinking water is one of the best ways to ensure good health, maintain and regulate the body's systems, and keep our immune system functioning well.

How much water do we need to drink? To maintain the most efficient and healthful body function, we need approximately one-half to three quarters ounces of water for every pound of body weight...that's 80 to 100 ounces of water if you weigh 160 pounds, or 8-10 glasses of water. Fluids like coffee or alcohol can actually cause the body to lose water and juices high in sugar contribute to dehydration and can increase the risk of kidney stones.

Water is the fuel that gives you energy to live. It lubricates joints and organs, maintains muscle tone, keeps skin soft, regulates body temperature, filters out impurities, and keeps our minds alert. It also carries important nutrients such as calcium, sodium, and potassium to cells. If you don't have enough water in your body, it can slow circulation and reduce concentration. You can retain more fluid if you don't have enough water in your system. Most of the fluids we lose each day go through the kidneys, which act like giant filters, filtering our blood twenty times every hour. Since human blood is 83% water, much of the kidney function has to do with filtering and disposing of water.

Drinking water can even aid in helping you lose weight because it can increase your metabolism. Try it. You'll be amazed! Drinking water helps clear up sinus conditions because it keeps the secretions thin, which allows them to flow more easily through the sinus passages. So for those of you who have tried all sorts of sinus medications, try drinking plenty of water and see if your sinuses feel better.

The reasons are endless why you need to drink water. Women who drink more than five glasses of water per day have been found to have fewer cases of heart disease and colon cancer. The risk was about half of what it was for women who drank less than two glasses a day. Water helps to regulate your body temperature and enhances physical and mental performance. Water helps prevent fatigue, headaches, and constipation.

If you want to improve your exercise routine or want to think more clearly, try drinking water! When you exercise, it is very important to make sure that you do not get dehydrated. If you are 1% dehydrated, you will become thirsty. The heat regulation in your body is now altered, and your performance has begun to decline. At 2% dehydration, there is increased thirst, and exercise becomes even more difficult. When you reach 5% dehydration, you can experience headaches, irritability, and that "spaced out" feeling that goes with extreme fatigue. At 6%, you become weaker and by 7% dehydration, you can collapse during exercise. So be careful. Drink water continually while you work out. Take a water bottle with you, and drink often while you exercise.

Think water. Drink water. If you include it in your everyday lifestyle, you will feel more energetic, and you will be doing your body a big favor.

LIMIT SWEETS

Sugar is a simple carbohydrate. It is considered to be the quickest energy source because it goes through the digestive system faster than any other carbohydrate. But white refined sugar, like in candy bars, cookies and soda, actually goes through the body too fast. It gives you a lot of energy all at once, but it doesn't stay in the body for very long. As quickly as it goes into your body, it goes out. That's when you start to feel tired and have less energy than before! And that's when you crave more sugar to give you that burst of energy once again. Your blood sugar will be far more even and balanced, though, if you exclude those foods high in white refined sugar.

Have you noticed that you have to eat a lot of sugar before you begin to feel full? Think about how you feel when you eat a piece of chocolate. Can you eat just one piece? You start to crave more and more. You don't get full on sweets like you do when you eat other foods. Can you eat more than one banana? Maybe you can eat two, but I bet you'll feel full afterward. Not so with sweets. They just don't fill you up.

You may not realize how much sugar you're actually eating, especially if you don't add it to your foods, but much of the sugar consumed is 'hidden' in foods. You just don't realize how much you are eating or drinking. If you get up in the morning and eat a bowl of sugared cereals, and I am talking about a small bowl, you have consumed four to six teaspoons of sugar. Then let's say on the way to work, you drink a soda. You drink one, then at work you drink another, then at lunch another. So you have three sodas in one day. That totals eight teaspoons in every soda, and you had three sodas during the day, so that equals 24 teaspoons of sugar. Now don't forget the six in the morning you ate in the cereal, a total of 30 teaspoons of white refined sugar. And that doesn't count the candy or doughnuts you might eat, or even the sugar in foods like salad dressing and ketchup! It is sometimes difficult to control the amount of sugar consumed, because we just don't realize how much we are eating.

Sugar also causes tooth decay. The bacteria in the mouth mix with the food that is eaten and gets between the teeth. When the bacteria digest the sugar, acid is produced. Acid is so strong that it eats away the tooth enamel, forming cavities. We can't replace our teeth once our baby teeth are gone, so we certainly don't want to let them rot!

Sugar comes in many forms, so when you see any of these foods on a label, there is some form of sugar in the product: sucrose, lactose, fructose, corn syrup, corn sweeteners, honey, dextrose, maple syrup, brown sugar, molasses, and raw sugar. Limit the white refined sugar to once a day, and you won't be overdoing it!

LIMIT SALT

Sodium, or in everyday language, salt, is a mineral, and everyone needs a little bit of it to keep the fluid in and around their cells in proper balance. The amount of salt you actually need each day is about 1/8 of a teaspoon, which is enough to cover your pinkie fingernail. One teaspoon, or about 2400 milligrams, is an acceptable amount. Try covering your smallest fingernail with salt and see how little that really is. Do you think you eat more salt than that every day?

Salt may affect blood pressure. High blood pressure, or hypertension, occurs when blood presses too hard against the artery walls. It can cause a stroke, heart problems, or kidney diseases. To really understand what high blood pressure does to your body, think of a balloon. When you blow it up halfway and squeeze it, nothing happens, but if you keep blowing it up, it will burst. It has too much pressure in it. You can't add too much pressure to a bicycle or an automobile tire, either, or it will burst. High blood pressure works the same way.

Our intake of salt comes from three major sources: **First, the salt that we add to food when we eat it or when we cook it.** It is estimated that about 25% of our salt comes from these foods. **Second, the salt added by the manufacturers of processed foods**. It is estimated that about 50% of our salt comes from these foods. Processed foods are foods that have been canned, frozen, put in boxes, or changed in any way from their natural state. Salt is in baking powder, baking soda, pickling solutions, and flavor enhancers. It is in medicines such as antacids, analgesics, and laxatives. If you eat hot dogs, pickles, soups, salted nuts, cheese spreads, lunch meats, ham, or "fast" foods, you are eating salt added by the manufacturers of processed foods. Any food that has salt listed as one of the first three ingredients is a high salt food. Many of our snack foods have a high salt content: potato chips, pretzels, tortilla chips, peanuts, and cheese. **Third, the salt in foods with a naturally high salt content.** About 25% of our salt comes from these foods. These foods are meat, chicken, turkey, fish, milk and cheese. They are rich sources of protein, calcium, iron and many other essential nutrients. You can't remove salt from these foods, but try to avoid adding extra salt.

If you cut back on high salty snacks, you will reduce at least some of your salt intake. You might ask, "Won't they be TASTELESS?" Not tasteless. Different. Your taste for extra salt is an acquired one, which can be un-acquired! Most people can easily adjust to using less salt in a couple of weeks. Sometimes it takes a little longer, but once the craving is gone, then it is gone!

THE WHERE...

Think about where you eat. Sometimes we just eat "wherever": in front of the TV, at fast food restaurants, or in the car on the way to work. We don't give it much thought. Years ago, it was the custom to sit down with the family and eat dinner. There was a regular time, and everyone was expected to be there. It was part of the American lifestyle. That custom has changed a lot with the faster pace of our world. Today, the children have soccer or football games after school; they take music and dance lessons. Teenagers drive their own cars and go out to fast food restaurants with their friends. Dinner is no longer on the table. It's leftovers in the refrigerator, pizza at the nearby pizzeria, or take out from the Chinese restaurant.

Where you eat determines at least part of your eating habits. If you sit in front of the TV, concentrating on the program and not on your food, you are doing yourself a big disservice. If you eat at fast food restaurants choosing triple hamburgers loaded with cheese and mayonnaise, it's going to affect your eating habits.

Eating should be for enjoyment, but it should also include wise decision making. The decision to eat healthy foods must come into play when you choose where you eat. Whether it is at a fast food restaurant or in your home, you should enjoy your meal. When you go to a fancy restaurant, you savor each bite. You probably talk about the food, how it tastes and how it smells. Part of the enjoyment of eating is the atmosphere that surrounds you, and you don't have to be in a fancy restaurant to make your eating environment something special. If it is at home, then light candles, put flowers on the table, turn on the stereo to soft dinner music. When you eat at a fast food restaurant, look at the menu; ask to see the nutrition breakdown of the food, and then look for a table that gives you a nice view. Give thought to the restaurant you choose. Is it pleasant to you? I know that I have walked into different fast food chains, and they each have their own atmosphere. Some are cleaner than others; some are quieter. You choose your environment. Don't let it choose you!

THE WHEN...

You have heard the expression, "Breakfast like a king, lunch like a prince and dinner like a pauper." It's true. The earlier in the day that you eat, the more time you will have to burn up those calories and not gain weight. I make it a policy not to eat anything after dinner. Once I get up from the table, I'm done for the night. A trick is to put a toothbrush and toothpaste in the closest bathroom to the kitchen. As soon as you get up from the table, before you do the dishes, brush your teeth. It will immediately cut your desire to eat more food.

Be conscious of when you eat certain foods and, more than likely, you will see a pattern. If the pattern is harmful to your health, then decide how you can adjust it. Do you have a routine concerning food, or do you eat at different times? What times of the day do you eat more than other times? Write down the times that you crave certain foods. You may find that you walk into the house at 5pm craving something sweet. It just may be that your blood sugar is too low, but if you eat some nuts and a piece of fruit at 4, you won't be as ravenous when you get home at 5.

Do you eat snacks? If so, when? Snacks can be healthy for you if you choose the healthy ones like fruits, nuts, or vegetables. If you are in the habit of eating high sugar foods and processed snacks, then it makes sense that they are not going to do you much good. They will probably leave you hungrier and craving more sweets. But if you can't do without your sweet snack, you might choose one snack a day that is healthy for you and one that you just can't live without. Don't think of eliminating all of those things that you love to eat. Just reduce the less healthy ones and increase the ones with more nutrients.

In conclusion, eat a big breakfast. You will have plenty of time to burn up those calories. Include whole wheat bread, yogurt, fresh fruit, or orange juice. Try whole wheat pancakes or bran muffins. Think whole grain. And think a lot of food for breakfast. Then think less for lunch, and even less for dinner. Throw in a few healthy snacks——-and you have it made!

THE HOW...

How do you change? It's not so complicated if you first understand how change occurs. Look at the following example. Jack is a friend who needs to change his eating habits because he just had a heart attack. If he doesn't start losing weight, he will most likely have to have a heart transplant. The doctor just told him that he has to make drastic lifestyle changes. Focus on the process that Jack has to go through in order to change his eating habits.

JACK...

"I've tried a million times to lose weight, and I end up gaining it instead! I have diabetes, a bad heart, and high blood pressure. I have to lose weight or else I could die! Maybe it's just hopeless."

STEP 1. WHAT IS THE SITUATION? Jack's problem is extreme. Yours, hopefully, is not as extreme, but it is important, nevertheless, to be aware of what the problem is. It could be that you need to lose weight, or that your cholesterol has been getting higher and higher, or that you don't have the energy you would like. Just being aware of your situation brings you to the next step.

STEP 2. WHAT DO YOU HAVE TO DO? Jack knows he has to change his eating habits. With this in mind, it is important for him to create a goal that is very specific. He may say that he wants to lose two pounds a week. You may need to cut calories to lose weight, eliminate the sugar in your diet because you were recently diagnosed with diabetes, or cut down on processed foods so that you don't have to go on high blood pressure medication.

STEP 3. WHY DO YOU WANT TO DO IT? Jack must want to make change. He can't just say it; he must be ready to do it. That's the hard part. He has his goal, which is to lose two pounds a week, but he must figure out something in his life that is so important that he is willing to change his eating habits because of it. That is the same for you. If you don't have an important reason to want to change, you won't change. Your reason can be that you want to fit into a dress for your daughter's wedding, or it can be that you want to reduce your chances of getting one of those nutrition related diseases that so many family members have, etc.

STEP 4. WHAT DO YOU NEED TO KNOW? Jack has to do some homework. So do you. Jack has to know about the foods that are healthy for him and those that are not. He will have to know how he can lose two pounds a week. There is no better way for him to make change than to understand as much about the food he eats as possible. He needs to ask his doctor about his cholesterol count, his EKG, and any other information about his heart. The more he knows, the more likely he will make the change. This is the time to read everything you can about your situation and the change you want to make. Become the expert. It doesn't have to be complicated information, but the more you know about the foods you eat that are unhealthy, and those you know you should eat, the more likely you will be to make a successful change.

5. WHAT ARE THE BENEFITS IF YOU MAKE THIS CHANGE SUCCESSFULLY? Jack needs to recognize the benefits if he eats properly. He may choose to do some visualization; that is to use his imagination to create what he wants in his life. He can visualize himself as a thin person, eating healthier foods. He can picture himself outside playing basketball with his children, energetic and happy. You can use visualization too. Create a mental picture in your mind. Think of your goal; imagine it in detail. Picture yourself eating healthy foods and enjoying them. What at first may seem impossible, becomes part of your everyday life.

6. FOCUS ON THE POSITIVE! Jack needs to focus on the positive. He should think about his goal and how much he wants to accomplish it. He needs to recognize when negative thoughts crop up, and get in the habit of replacing them with positive thoughts. This is a drastic change for many people, but is successful if done on a day by day basis. Take just one day, and each time a negative thought comes to mind, mentally picture a stop sign in front of your face. Then take a moment to replace that negative thought with a positive one instead. Each time you are successful with this technique, give yourself a pat on the back. If you can get away from negative thoughts and start to look at yourself and your situation in a positive manner, you will be creating a new behavior that will most certainly help you to be a winner!

Now it's your turn to work through this process.

STEP 1. WHAT IS MY SITUATION?

_____
_____
_____

STEP 2. WHAT DO I HAVE TO DO?

_____
_____

STEP 3. WHY DO I WANT TO DO IT?

_____
_____
_____

STEP 4. WHAT DO I NEED TO KNOW?

_____
_____
_____

STEP 5. WHAT ARE THE BENEFITS IF I MAKE THE CHANGE SUCCESSFULLY?

_____
_____
_____

STEP 6. HOW DO I FOCUS ON THE POSTIVE?

_____
_____
_____

STEP 7. YOU ARE THE WINNER!

MY FOUR QUARTERS EATING PLAN

It's easy to follow. Start slowly. Take sixteen weeks to do it. Each four weeks is one quarter. I guarantee you will change your eating habits.

WEEK ONE——Eat more vegetables this week. Read the section on vegetables in this chapter. Each day, increase your consumption of vegetables. That's all you have to do this week. Think and eat vegetables. Your choice! Choose the ones that you like, and then experiment. Try to eat as many different color vegetables as possible. Eat vegetables of different shapes and textures. Think color, texture, shape.

WEEK TWO——Eat fresh fruit every day this week. Read the section on fruit in this chapter. Drink fruit juices, but make sure they are pure juice and not filled with sugar. Eat fruits of different colors. Eat a piece of fruit in the morning. Think fruit and continue with the vegetables.

WEEK THREE——Drink water this week. Read the information on water in this chapter. Increase the amount of water you drink every day this week. If you don't drink any water, drink one glass the first day, then two the second and so on. Substitute water for soda. Soon you will see that you will crave water. Try to reach a goal of at least seven glasses of water a day.

WEEK FOUR——Begin to eat whole grain breads. Read the information about whole grains in this chapter. Become an expert on why whole grains are important to your health. By the end of the week eat at least two pieces of whole wheat bread daily. Go to the supermarket and look at all of the different kinds of grains. There is Ukrainian rye bread, seven grain whole wheat bread, pumpernickel. Think dark bread is good! Eat whole grain cereal for breakfast this week. If you don't like whole grain cereal, then eat whole grain bread for breakfast, or try whole wheat pancakes. Just think whole grain. Continue eating your fruits and vegetables, and don't forget to drink that water!

This ends the first quarter. By the end of this quarter you should be in the habit of thinking vegetables, fruits and whole grains. You should be eating these regularly, and you should also have increased the water you drink. Give yourself a pat on the back! The hardest part is over. Now you know that you can make change. You are doing it. You are on the right track.

WEEK FIVE—Think about when you eat. Keep a journal that shows the times of day that you eat. Remember, you should eat your biggest meal in the morning. Lunch should be lighter than breakfast, but not as light as dinner. Snacks should be small and filled with nutrients. This is the week to focus on when you eat. Keep up with your fruits, vegetables, and whole grains. And drink plenty of water!

WEEK SIX— Eliminate the white bread and white pasta. If you are used to white bread and white pasta, the whole wheat brands may taste too grainy for you. Try Jerusalem artichoke pasta. It tastes like the white spaghetti. You can buy it in the supermarket. There are all kinds of varieties of pasta and bread that have a whole grain base. Review the material on whole grains in this chapter.

WEEK SEVEN—Eat fish, especially salmon, albacore tuna, anchovies or mackerel. Read the information about increasing the good fats in your diet, which includes fatty fish. Broil or bake the fish. Go to the fish section of your supermarket and buy a fresh piece of salmon. Fish is inexpensive. Try different recipes. Look on the web for interesting ideas. Type in fish or salmon, and you will get a wide assortment of recipes. You don't have to buy a new cookbook. Be creative with your meals. If you eat at a restaurant, order broiled or baked salmon, blackened tuna, or grilled mackerel.

WEEK EIGHT— Reduce the red meat; eat turkey or chicken, but make sure it is without the skin, and keep to the white meat. Read the information about cholesterol so you know why you should reduce red meat in your diet. You don't have to eliminate the red meat, just reduce the amount. Think about eating red meat no more than once a week. The other days concentrate on fish and poultry. Don't forget the legumes, such as soybeans, black beans, split peas and lentils! They are a great substitute for meat.

This completes the second quarter. You are at half time now! You have accomplished a lot in these eight weeks. By now you should be accustomed to eating vegetables, fruits and whole grains. You are eating more fish and poultry. You have reduced the red meat for one week, so you are on the way toward a healthier diet.

WEEK NINE—Eliminate foods with Trans fatty acids. Read the information about Trans fatty acids so you know what you need to eliminate. Start reading food labels. If the product has partially hydrogenated oil in it...don't eat it. Choose snacks that are fresh, not processed. When you read a label, recognize that the ingredients go in the order of the amount of that particular ingredient in the product. So if the first ingredient is sugar, than there is more sugar in the product than anything else. Become an expert label reader. Look at the grams of fat too. How many grams are saturated?

WEEK TEN—It's time to start including those good fats and good oils into your body. Put olive oil on your bread. Eliminate the butter and margarine. Use safflower oil in your cooking. Buy salad dressing that has olive oil in it, or use plain olive oil with balsamic vinegar. Think good oils this week. No butter. No lard. Nuts and seeds are healthy snacks and have the good fat that you need. Eat almonds, walnuts, and sunflower seeds. You don't have to eat bags of them. Eat six almonds at a time, a handful of walnuts, or two handfuls of sunflower seeds. Don't think calories. Your body needs these fats, and if you eat a healthy diet, you will not gain weight from these foods.

WEEK ELEVEN—This week focus on where you eat. If you eat many meals at restaurants, think about whether those restaurants offer foods that will improve your health. If you eat most of your meals at home, make sure that you eat them at the kitchen or dining room table. Set the table. Make it a habit to sit down and enjoy the food. If you eat with your family, this is time that is very important for socializing and bonding together. Make your meals a pleasant experience.

WEEK TWELVE—Limit sweets to one a day. Your choice. You can choose what sweet you want to eat, but only one sweet a day. That means if you eat pancakes with syrup for breakfast, that's your sweet for the day. ONE SWEET A DAY. Read the information on what sugar does to your body in the Sweet Section of this chapter.

The third quarter is over. You are well on your way toward a healthy diet. If you have followed this plan for twelve weeks, you must be feeling more energetic and proud! Keep it up! The fourth quarter gets even better!

WEEK THIRTEEN—Eat a big breakfast every day this week. It should include whole grains, fruit or fruit juice, and yogurt or skim milk. Walk away from the table satisfied, but not stuffed. On a scale of 1-10, with 10 being Thanksgiving kind of stuffed, you should never go over a 5 when you walk away from the table. You should feel full and satisfied, but not stuffed!

WEEK FOURTEEN—Reduce the cholesterol. Remember, our bodies need some cholesterol, but not too much. Review the information about cholesterol in this chapter. The more knowledge you have about cholesterol and what it does to your body, the more likely you will be to choose foods that won't raise your cholesterol level. By now, the cholesterol you are consuming should be low, but just in case it is still high, reduce those foods that are particularly high in cholesterol this week: organ meat such as brains, kidney, liver, egg yolk, fatty meats, shrimp, butter, lard, cream, whole milk and whole milk cheeses. Since you still need to get calcium from milk products, emphasize those that have less fat: skim milk and skim milk cheeses. Look on the label at the milligrams of cholesterol. Two milligrams of cholesterol per serving is a low cholesterol food.

WEEK FIFTEEN—Limit processed foods that are high in salt to one a day. Read the label. Remember, you don't need more than 2400 milligrams of salt in a day...and that is a high figure! Read the information about salt in this chapter. Become familiar with the foods that are high in salt. Experiment with spices that you can use instead of using the salt shaker.

WEEK SIXTEEN—This week, focus on your portion sizes. A portion size of meat should be no larger than a deck of cards. Don't overeat! If you are choosing healthy foods, more than likely you are not eating too much. Remember that you can eat vegetables in abundance. If you concentrate on the vegetables, fruits and whole grains, then you will be filling up on foods that provide you with an abundance of nutrients.

Congratulate yourself! You have made significant changes in your eating habits.

If there were weeks that were difficult for you, just start those weeks over again. Everyone makes change at a different pace. You are well on your way to better health!

Now that you have completed the plan, think about your results. How do you feel? Do you know more about yourself and your eating habits than you did sixteen weeks ago? What do you still need to change? It's not easy to change our eating habits. It is a life long process. We have advertisements that try to make us want things that may not be the best for us. We have menus in restaurants that have foods on them that seem very appealing. We go to parties and are surrounded by less than healthy fare, foods high in the wrong kinds of fat, high in sugar, high in salt.

There are so many distractions that can interfere with our goals. To focus takes discipline, and only you can provide that discipline for yourself. But I guarantee if you choose healthy foods, the benefits you'll reap will be so wonderful that you won't want to go back to your old ways. You'll feel more energetic. You will be less at risk for those nutrition related disease, and you will age with grace and dignity, looking forward to the next quarter of life!

FOUR QUARTERS EATING PLAN								
FIRST QUARTER	**WHAT I NEED TO DO**	**I DID IT**						
		S	M	T	W	Th	F	S
WEEK ONE								
WEEK TWO								
WEEK THREE								
WEEK FOUR								
SECOND QUARTER								
WEEK ONE								
WEEK TWO								
WEEK THREE								
WEEK FOUR								
THIRD QUARTER								
WEEK ONE								
WEEK TWO								
WEEK THREE								
WEEK FOUR								
FOURTH QUARTER								
WEEK ONE								
WEEK TWO								
WEEK THREE								
WEEK FOUR								

PHYSICAL EXERCISE

PHYSICAL EXERCISE

In 1995, a Harris Poll asked people to list their favorite free time activities; 38% of the people chose dancing, bowling, walking, doing yard work, etc. They did something that involved exercise. In 2003, that number dropped to 29%. Unless we start to make a conscious effort to add activity into our daily lives, that number will continue to drop. As it drops, so does our health. A sedentary lifestyle does not produce a healthy body and mind.

Lack of exercise is one of the leading causes of obesity. The number of obese people in the US has grown to more than 44 million people. That number has doubled from 15% in 1980 to 31% in 2000 according to the Centers for Disease Control and Prevention in Atlanta. Men are slightly more likely to be obese than women, and people in their third quarter of life are more likely to be overweight than those who are younger.

An associate public health professor at the University of North Carolina at Chapel Hill, Rich Killingsworth, said that our society is divided into roughly three groups. About 25% of us stay fit. You know those people. They won't miss a day at the gym. They walk in all kinds of weather. Fitness is part of their life routine. Then there are another 25% who do nothing. They don't exercise at all. It's the other 50% that go back and forth. They are the ones who have become less active in recent years.

Federal health officials and our government are trying hard to change this trend. They emphasize different types of physical exercise, recommending at least twenty minutes of vigorous activity such as swimming laps, power walking, jogging, or chopping wood at least three times a week. They say you can get similar benefits from moderate activity including brisk walking, dancing or bicycling for 30 minutes a day, five days a week.

People spend hours watching TV, working on the computer, playing video games, and watching sports. These activities require no physical exertion. When you think about mowing your lawn, do you hand mow it or do you have a riding mower? We have many conveniences to make our lives easier: automatic car windows, elevators, escalators– everything for convenience, but this convenience is hurting us.

We need to become more active. The Gameplan for Aging places great emphasis on the lifestyle factors that affect aging. Each one is as important as the next, and each one affects the others. That's the theme throughout this book, but exercise is probably the most important thing you can do for yourself to age the way most of you would like. It's important to keep active, both physically and mentally.

Challenge yourself a little. You'll have more fun in life, and you will feel better. Sure, there may be genetic factors, but don't minimize your lifestyle if you don't have to.

Now let's look at physical exercise. Why is it so important for you to exercise? You probably have heard these reasons before, but let's go over them in relation to the Gameplan for Aging. This next section will be interactive. You'll have to participate for it to work for you. So get out a pen and enjoy. It's all about you!

WHY EXERCISE?

Physical exercise has many benefits. You can reduce your risk of dying prematurely by almost 50% if you exercise almost every day, because physical exercise cuts the risk of high blood pressure, heart attacks, diabetes, osteoporosis, stroke, depression, and anxiety. If you are physically fit, you strengthen your bones. How many older people do you know who have broken a hip or have fallen and broke a leg? Exercise gives us other benefits as well. You'll have more energy, you'll control your weight, possibly lower your cholesterol, and increase your metabolism. You will look better and be stronger. You'll have more endurance, decrease your risk of colds, and have less sick days from work.

You'll also sleep better, reduce your stress, and will be able to deal with problems in a healthier way. You will reduce anxiety and improve your mood. You will feel better about yourself and have more confidence. You will be more focused. Your memory will improve. Your anger will decrease and you will be more efficient. Enough reasons??????

There is no doubt, your life changes when you exercise. Your body was made to move around. Just as a river flows and would become stagnant without movement, your body needs to move. The quality of our life is affected by our mobility or immobility.

We are going to cover three different types of exercise: aerobic, muscular strength training and stretching. Let's examine each of them.

AEROBIC EXERCISE

An exercise is aerobic if it raises your heart level for a sustained period of time. Aerobic exercise burns calories and increases your metabolic rate so that you burn calories more efficiently throughout the day. Aerobic exercise can lower blood pressure, reduce stress, and strengthen your heart and lungs.

Before you can consider an aerobic exercise program, you must know something about your physical condition. Let's start with your heart rate. It will affect what aerobic exercise you can do and how hard you should do it.

Count your heart beats for 20 seconds. Multiply that number by 3 to find your heart rate per minute. Record your heart rate in the morning, during a break in your day, and then again at night. When you start an exercise routine, your heart rate may change. An average heart rate is usually between 72 and 80 beats per minute, but this can vary. Ask your doctor what a healthy heart rate is for you.

The approximate recommended heart rate is different for people of different ages and different health status. Remember, an average resting heart rate is usually between 72-80 beats per minute.

AGE	AEROBIC TRAINING RATE
20	160
25	155
30	152
35	148
40	146
45	143
50	140
55	137
60	128
65+	120

Record your heart rate.

MY HEART RATE:

MORNING_____

MID-MORNING_____

NIGHT_____

Do you know your aerobic fitness level? What do you think it is?

Great _____ Not very good

| 1 | 2 | 3 | 4 | 5 | 6 | 7 | 8 |

Can you walk 1/2 mile?_____
One mile?_____
Two miles?_____
Run one mile?_____

MY TARGET HEART RATE AND MY HEART RECOVERY RATE

You also need to know your target heart rate and your heart recovery rate. There is a lower and upper level Maximum Heart Rate. You should NEVER exceed the upper level. Target heart rates often need to be adjusted for certain individuals. Some people naturally have a higher or lower heart rate.

To get your target heart rate,
Lower level= (220 – your age) x .60. So if you are 50 years old—(220 – 50= 170). Take the 170 x.60 =102 beats per minute.

Higher level= (220 – your age) x .90. If you are 50 years old—(220 – 50= 170. Take the 170 x .90 = 153 beats per minute.

So the target heart rate of a 50 year old who is exercising should be between 102 and 153 beats per minute.

Now take your pulse again, just like you did before, to get your heart rate while you're exercising. It should be in your target range.

It is important to know how quickly your heart recovers after exercise. Count your pulse five minutes after you exercise. If it's above 115 beats per minute, you were overdoing it. After 10 minutes it should be below 100. Take your pulse before, during, and after an exercise routine.

MY HEART RATE:

AT REST _____

DURING EXERCISE _____

AFTER EXERCISE _____

CALORIES USED IN EXERCISE

Different activities burn different amounts of calories. The chart below gives the calories used per hour in different activities.

Approximate Energy Expenditure by a 150 Pound Person In Various Activities

Activity	Calories Per Hour
Lying down or sleeping	80
Sitting	100
Driving an automobile	120
Standing	140
Domestic work	180
Walking, 4km/hour	210
Bicycling, 8.8km/hour	210
Gardening	220
Lawn mowing, power mower	250
Walking, 6km/hour	300
Volleyball	300
Swimming, .4km/hour	300
Folk dancing, roller skating	350
Weight training	350
Tennis	420
Skiing, 16km/hour	600
Basketball	600
Soccer	650
Bicycling, 20.8km/hour	660
Running, 16km/hour	900

For every pound of muscle you gain, you burn 50 more calories than a pound of fat.

MUSCULAR STRENGTH TRAINING

The second type of exercise is muscular strength training. This includes: weight training, sit-ups, pull-ups, push-ups, and chin-ups. These exercises do not rely on oxygen like aerobic exercises do. They build muscle mass. They require short intense bursts of energy. One component of your physical fitness is your ability to use your muscles and not let them get weak. A muscle becomes stronger when it is worked at higher levels. It is important to have the proper technique when you strength train so that you reduce your chance of injury. These exercises are important for you as you age because they help strengthen your muscles and bones.

Take a few minutes now to see your muscular strength training level.

MY STRENGTHS

Date _____

Number of sit-ups I can do_____

Number of pull-ups I can do_____

Number of push-ups I can do_____

Number of chin-ups I can do_____

Weight training that I do_____

STRETCHING

Stretching has many long-term benefits. It reduces depression, anxiety, anger and fatigue, and takes only minutes. It will help you feel better throughout the day. It isn't hard to stretch, but there is a right and wrong way to do it. The right way is to stretch slowly and to focus on the muscles you are stretching. It is wrong to bounce or push the stretch to the point that it is painful.

The following are examples of just a few stretches you can do almost anywhere, even on the job. Give these a try. Not only will you feel better, but if done on a regular basis, you'll also become more aware of your body. This can lead you to become motivated to keep your body healthy and strong through exercise and proper nutrition.

Another surprising benefit of stretching is safety. Studies have proven that employees who have a stretching program at work also have far less injuries. This extends to home as well, with less injuries reported from weekend sports, home improvement projects, etc.

Separate and straighten your fingers until tension of a stretch is felt (fig.1). Hold for 10 seconds. Relax, then bend your fingers at the knuckles and hold for 10 seconds (fig.2). Repeat stretch in fig. 1 once more.

Interlace your fingers in front of you and rotate your hands and wrists clockwise 10 times. Repeat counter-clockwise 10 times. This will improve flexibility of hands and wrists and provide a slight warm-up.

With fingers interlaced behind head, keep elbows straight out to side with upper body in a good aligned position. Pull your shoulder blades toward each other to create a feeling of tension through upper back and shoulder blades. Hold this feeling of mild tension for 8-10 seconds, then relax. Do several times.

With fingers interlaced behind your back, slowly turn your elbows inward while straightening your arms. This is good to do when you find yourself slumping forward from your shoulders. Hold for 5-15 seconds. Do twice.

WHICH EXERCISE IS RIGHT FOR ME?

Now it's time for you to think about the exercise that is right for you. You should include all three types into an exercise program. Choose activities that you'll enjoy, because if you don't like to do something, chances are you won't stick with it. Look at the list below. Cross out those exercises that immediately "turn you off" or you can't do, or won't do, for one reason or another.

Activity				
Domestic Work	Bicycling	Walking	Gardening	Canoeing
Golf	Lawn mowing	Bowling	Fencing	Row boating
Swimming	Fast Walking	Badminton	Horseback riding	Dancing
Volleyball	Roller skating	Table tennis	Ice skating	Pilates
Tennis	Water skiing	Hill climbing (100 ft./hour)	Skiing	Squash and handball
Scull rowing	Running	Weights	Stretching	Sit-ups
Push-ups	Free weights	Hiking	Yoga	Martial Arts

Look at this list and see whether you have chosen exercises that fit into the three categories.

Sample List

	Aerobic Exercise	Muscle Strength and Endurance	Stretching
Aerobic Step	x	x	x
Bicycling	x	x	
Gardening		x	
Golf	x	x	
Jogging	x	x	
Swimming	x	x	
Lifting Weights		x	x
Walking	x		
Yoga	x		x
Stretching			x

Which aerobic exercises do you like?

_____

Which muscular strength training exercises do you like?

_____

Are you stretching?

_____

Now that you know which exercises you like to do, you need to know how exercise affects your body. Some people get that exercise "high" and can't live without it. Others never like the exercise they do; they do it because "they have to!" If you are aware of what exercise does for you, you will be more likely to stick with an exercise program.

EXERCISE AWARENESS

Take five minutes and walk, stretch, run, or do sit-ups. Think of the following. How does your body feel?

How does your body feel?	Comfortable	Uncomfortable
Your breathing		
Your shoulders		
Your legs		
Your feet		
Your posture		
Your muscles and joints		
Your knees		

How do you feel mentally when you exercise? Are you frustrated because you don't want to spend the time? Are you bored or do you feel invigorated? It is important for you to be aware of how you feel, and it is best for your health to feel good about what you are doing. If you don't feel good about the activity, you will either stop doing it, or you won't get the full benefits. Remember, the lifestyle factors all work together. Your attitude affects your exercise, which affects your sleep, which affects your lifestyle, and so on.

For now, just think about how exercise makes you feel. How did you feel the last time you were exercising?

Energetic	Bored
Happy	Annoyed
Challenged	Peaceful
Satisfied	Frustrated
Sluggish	Depressed

In order to really develop an exercise program, you need to think about the emotional triggers in your life. You may ask, "What does one thing have to do with another?" I've heard too many people say that they hate to exercise. They get frustrated when they're working out, and they don't reap the benefits.

I disagree with that thinking. You don't just get frustrated when you walk, for example. You're carrying around that frustration before you even start out Something in your life is triggering you to feel that way. You don't have to resolve that emotion right now, but think about what triggers you to feel the way you do. Then ask yourself: Does this really have anything to do with the exercise? For instance, if your boss is on your back, and you are frustrated, then when you exercise, is that frustration still with you? Think about the emotional triggers in your life.

What makes you frustrated at work?

_____

_____

What makes you frustrated about your relationship with your friends?

_____

_____

What makes you frustrated with your spouse?

_____

_____

What makes you frustrated with your children?

_____

_____

Do you get frustrated with politics?

_____

_____

What other frustrations do you have?

_____

_____

Do you feel frustrated when you exercise?

_____

_____

How can you separate your frustrations from your workout?

_____

_____

THE RIGHT EXERCISE FOR ME

When you consider an exercise program, there are other factors. Who you are affects your exercise routine. If you love physical adventure, you're more likely to succeed if your exercise routine includes hiking the Appalachian Trail one day and biking through the city the next, rather than walking the same route day after day.

I have friends who have chosen the wrong exercise routine and others who know exactly what works for them. John, a good friend, decided as a New Year's Resolution to go to the gym every other day and lift weights. I knew it wouldn't last. I talked with him.

"John, do you think you'll keep this routine up?" I asked.

"This time, I believe I will. I got a bad report from the doctor," he replied.

"Is a bad report enough motivation for you to keep it up?"

"I think it should be, Mark," he replied.

"I know you want to build up body mass, but for some reason, I have my doubts," I told him. I felt guilty saying that to John, but something nagged inside of me when I thought of John's personality. John loves people. He doesn't like to be alone, so the gym was a good starting point, and John likes competition so that seemed to fit too. But what didn't seem to fit was that John was going to the gym, working out on weights by himself, and making a commitment to do it every other day. John also loves the outdoors and doesn't like to be inside, so that didn't fit. He does not have good time management skills, either, so no one was going to be there to push him to get to the gym.

I suggested that John find an exercise routine that involved other people, such as tennis. In nice weather he could play outdoors, so he wouldn't always have to be inside. If he played with someone, he would have to be there for the game. He's a reliable guy when it comes to others, so I knew that if he made the commitment to someone else, he would be there. John and I talked for awhile, and he realized that the type of exercise he chose was an important factor in his commitment to keeping it up. It was important for him to be outdoors at least some of the time.

Some people like the indoors and some like the outdoors. Another friend, Ron, walks every day. We live on the east coast and sometimes the weather is not conducive for outdoor activities, but Ron loves to walk outside. It doesn't matter if it's five degrees below zero; Ron is out there walking seven miles every morning. He just bundles up. He's read several books about walking and even thought about writing one of his own some day. He's aware of what he should wear when he walks, the speed he should walk, and how to choose his route. Ron walks when it's 90 degrees, too. He knows to take a water bottle. If it's too hot, he gets up at 5am to get the walk in before the heat of the day. He'll do whatever's necessary. You can't put Ron on a treadmill. He has to be outdoors.

WHERE SHOULD I EXERCISE?

Visualize the place that you feel most comfortable. Is it in a gym among strangers or in a dance class with friends? Do you like to be outdoors no matter what the weather? Rank the places listed below from 1-5 with 5 being great. Decide on an exercise program based on the "5's"!

HOME_____

FITNESS CENTER _____

OUTSIDE_____

POOL _____

OTHER_____

CHOOSING THE RIGHT EXERCISE

Look at the statements below. Think about the type of person you are and what kind of exercise routine fits your personality.

Put a T for True next to those statements that describe you...and an F for False for those that do not.

	True	False
1. I like to workout with other people.		
2. I am a competitive person.		
3. I like to workout alone.		
4. I am athletic.		
5. I prefer to exercise outside.		
6. I like to go camping.		
7. I like adventure.		
8. I prefer winter sports.		
9. I get bored easily.		
10. I like organized sports.		
11. I love to take risks.		
12. I love to sweat.		
13. I need a schedule in order to get things done.		
14. I am flexible.		
15. I like routine.		
16. It is easy for me to set goals.		
17. I love the water.		
18. I am not interested in sports.		
19. I enjoy walking.		
20. I like to try new things.		

WHEN SHOULD I EXERCISE?

It's important to think about when to exercise. If you are a morning person, you might want to exercise in the morning. If you are a night person, the late afternoon might be just fine for you. Ron's son, Dan, is a night owl. He is a writer and writes into the wee hours of the morning. No one could get Dan to exercise until his dad said, "Why don't you go at night? You don't go to sleep until 4am on a typical night, so you could be the last one in the swimming pool just before it closes." So now Dan is the last one in the pool...and he swims because he has chosen the best times for him.

What days are best for you to exercise? Try to choose 3-5 days	
Sunday	
Monday	
Tuesday	
Wednesday	
Thursday	
Friday	
Saturday	

When are your best hours? Think about what type of person you are (a morning or night person) and consider your schedule as well. Try to decide upon a time that fits your needs. How do you feel at each of these times? What time do you think is best for you to exercise?

8am	_____
9am	_____
10am	_____
11am	_____
12pm	_____
1pm	_____
2pm	_____
3pm	_____
4pm	_____
5pm	_____
6pm	_____
7pm	_____
8pm	_____
9pm	_____
10pm	_____
11pm	_____
12pm	_____
1am	_____
2am	_____
3am	_____
4am	_____
5am	_____
6am	_____
7am	_____

Many of you may say, "But I still don't have the time." That seems to be a major problem in our busy world. So what can you do about it? How do you find TIME to exercise? You just don't have another second to add anything to your schedule. You may find that you really can do more than you think, though. Refer to the section on Time Management to help you manage your time.

MY FOUR QUARTERS EXERCISE PLAN

WHY DO I WANT TO EXERCISE?

_____

_____

_____

_____

WHICH TYPE OF EXERCISE DO I PREFER?
  Aerobic _____
  Muscular Strength Training _____
  Stretching _____
  All of the above_____

WHERE WILL I EXERCISE?

_____

_____

_____

_____

WHEN IS THE BEST TIME FOR ME TO EXERCISE?

_____

_____

_____

_____

WHAT IS MY TARGET HEART RATE?

_____

_____

OTHER IMPORTANT INFORMATION I NEED IN
ORDER TO DEVELOP AN EXERCISE PROGRAM

_____

_____

_____

MENTAL FITNESS

We can improve our minds just as we can improve our physical bodies. There are several things that you can do, at any age, to strengthen your mind. Years ago, when we relied on IQ tests, people were boxed into a certain intelligence quotient. Today we know more about the brain and how it affects our thinking.

WHOLE BRAIN THINKING

Whole brain thinking occurs when we use both the left and right hemispheres of our brain, but for many of us, one side of the brain is usually stronger. Answer the following questions. Choose the first answer that comes to your mind. If you can't decide, choose the one that you do more often than the other.

1. When you have something important to do, do you ...
    A. Get nervous or tense
    B. Just let things happen

2. Do you often feel sad?
    A. No
    B. Yes

3. When listening to music, which do you like better?
    A. The beat
    B. The melody

4. Which method of learning works best for you?
   A. Books and lectures
   B. Interactive workshops and group activities

5. Which do you prefer?
   A. Math, science
   B. Art, music

6. How do you get everything accomplished in your day?
   A. Organize all details and know exactly what you plan to do.
   B. Go with the flow.

7. When you plan to go away, how thorough are you in making sure
   that you have everything you need?
   A. Yes, I check and double check everything.
   B. If something is missing, I improvise.

8. How do you organize your day if you have errands to run?
   A. I make a list, writing down everywhere I have to go inorder.
   B. I just go from place to place.

9. Which type of puzzle do you prefer?
   A. Crossword puzzle
   B. Jigsaw puzzle

10. When you exercise, how do you do it?
    A. The same time each day, same workout schedule from
       week to week.
    B. When I feel like it and have the time. It varies.

11. Is it easy for you to remember names?
    A. Yes
    B. No

12. Is it easy for you to remember faces?
    A. Yes
    B. No

13. If you need to go somewhere you've never been, do you
    A. Ask for directions, and write them down
    B. Look at a map

14. How do you feel about alternative medicine?
    A. It's not scientific
    B. It could work for me

15. Do you enjoy taking risks?
    A. No
    B. Yes

16. Do you usually know the time without looking at your watch?
    A. Yes
    B. No

17. Do you prefer working alone or in a group?
    A. Alone
    B. Group

18. Do you prefer scheduled social events?
    A. Yes
    B. No

19. Clasp your hands comfortably. Which thumb is on top?
    A. Left
    B. Right

20. Would you say you're a very organized person?
    A. Yes
    B. No

Count your A's and B's. If you have more A's, you are more of a left brain thinker. If you have more B's, you are more of a right brain thinker. The left side of the brain is: analytical, linear, explicit, sequential, verbal, concrete, rational, and goal oriented. The right brain hemisphere is the part of our brain that is: intuitive, emotional, nonverbal, visual, artistic, holistic, playful, symbolic, and physical.

So who cares, you might ask. When we use both hemispheres of our brain, we are mentally more alert. When we are mentally more alert, we age in a healthier way. We can affect the aging process by stimulating both hemispheres of our brain. For some of you who are more left brained than right brained, there are mental exercises that you can do to strengthen the right side of the brain. The reverse is true for those of you who are more right brained. These exercises won't take time away from your day. You can even include them into your daily routine.

For those of you who want to strengthen the right side of your brain, try the following:

1. Look at the big picture. Instead of the details. If you are super organized, instead of making up a list and following through with all the details, look at the overall picture. What is the most important thing for you to get done? Discover patterns in your work style.
2. Respond to body language. Someone can be telling you a lot just by how they smile, laugh, or clasp their hands together. Notice what they are expressing non verbally. Focus on their tone of voice. What does it show you?
3. Visualize something. For example, let's say that you want to walk faster. Instead of reading a book about how to walk faster, visualize yourself walking faster. Think of your body, how it looks, how it feels. You can even daydream that you are in a competition, and you are the fastest walker.
4. Expand your vocabulary. Use colorful and playful words.
5. Feel someone elses point of view.
6. Move around, exercise, play, and enjoy yourself.

7. Sing or hum.
8. Take a walk for no special reason.
9. Visualize colors. For example, visualize greens and blues. Feel the coolness.
10. Shift your phone from your right ear to your left for emphatic listening; *that is feeling what the person is saying.*
11. Be aware of colors, space, smells, sounds, and feelings that surround you.
12. Become a doodler.
13. Breathe deeply.
14. Close your eyes, daydream for a few minutes.
15. Make eye contact with others. How are they feeling.
16. Look at the whole situation.

For those of you who want to strengthen the left side of your brain, try the following:

1. Make lists.
2. Organize; prioritize what you need to do in a day.
3. Set goals.
4. Try to stick to your decisions.
5. Shift your phone to your right ear for analytic reasoning.
6. Make outlines.
7. Do crossword puzzles.
8. Solve math problems.
9. Think of the colors amber and yellow to slow down. Feel the warmth.
10. Play chess.
11. Keep a journal.
12. Take up an instrument.
13. Try a new hobby.
14. Make a list to plan your day.
15. Be aware of time.
16. Make a schedule and stick to it.
17. Break a problem into separate parts. Don't just look at the whole picture. Try looking at the details.

There are more things to consider when you think of becoming mentally fit. How do you learn best? Each person has a style of learning that is most comfortable for him/her. We get into our comfort zones and it helps us in life, but when we are too comfortable in that zone, it can actually inhibit brain stimulation. Let's look at your style of learning. Are you a visual learner? Do you learn best by seeing the information? Or are you an auditory learner? Do you prefer to hear the information? Perhaps you are an kinesthetic learner? Do you prefer to touch and explore the information?

WHAT'S MY LEARNING STYLE?

These questions will take less than five minutes to answer. As you answer them, think about how you can improve the weaker styles of your learning. Don't give too much thought. Your first reaction is usually the way you would do it.

1. Which would you prefer?
   A. A book with pictures
   B. A book with stories about people
   C. A book where you answer questions and do puzzles
      (interactive)

2. How would you prefer to learn about something new?
   A. Watch a movie about it
   B. Listen to someone explain it
   C. Touch, experience it

3. If you aren't sure about the spelling of a word, which of these are you most likely to do?
   A. Write it down and look at it
   B. Sound it out
   C. Write it out to sense if it feels right

4. When you meet new people, do you remember...
    A. Faces, but not names
    B. Names, but not faces
    C. The things people say

5. How do you prefer to learn new information?
    A. Read notes, look at diagrams, illustrations
    B. Have someone ask you questions, or repeat facts silently
       to yourself
    C. Write things out on index cards, make diagrams, models,
       illustrations

6. When you see a word like, cholesterol, what do you do first?
    A. Think of a picture: ex. an artery clogged with fat
    B. Say the word, 'cholesterol' to yourself silently
    C. Sense how it would feel to have a clogged artery

7. When you are making dinner, what is most distracting to you?
    A. Visual distractions such as the television
    B. Noises such as loud music or someone screaming
    C. Sensations like hunger, etc.

8. How do you plan your day?
    A. Make a list and check items off as they are done
    B. Just go with the flow
    C. Go through the days events in your mind

9. How do you prefer to spend a Sunday afternoon?
    A. An art museum
    B. A concert
    C. A hike in the woods

10. If you go to a play, or concert, what do you do when you first walk
    into the lobby?
    A. Look around to find a program that will give you an
       explanation of the event.
    B. Talk to other people about the event.
    C. Go into the theatre or auditorium, find something interest
       ing to look at, and read the agenda later.

11. When you are angry at someone, what are you likely to do?
     A. Make an angry face
     B. Shout at the person
     C. Stomp off and say nothing

12. Which would you rather do?
     A. Look at a painting.
     B. Listen to music.
     C. Exercise.

13. How would you prefer to tell a story?
     A. Write it.
     B. Tell it out loud.
     C. Act it out.

14. When you listen to music, do you
     A. Close your eyes and see pictures that go with the music.
     B. Hum along with the music.
     C. Move with the music.

15. If you have to teach something to a child, which would you prefer to do?
     A. Show illustrations
     B. Read information out loud
     C. Do something practical to teach him/her.

Count your A's, B's and C's. If you have more A's, you are a VISUAL learner and learn best by seeing the information. If you have more B's, you are an AUDITORY learner and prefer to hear the information. If you have more C's, you are a KINESTHETIC learner. You prefer to touch and explore the information.

If you are a visual learner, to stay mentally fit, you might try to expand your auditory skills. That may mean, simply, that you should try to listen more carefully. Some of these activities can easily be fit into your life, and as you fit them in, you are improving your mental alertness...and your aging process.

If you are a visual learner, you may use more visual words. When you describe something, do you say: *picture that...focus on this...* Do you use words like: *see, bright, clear, glimpse*? If you are an auditory learner do you use words like: *note, ring, shout, sing, heard, scream, ask,* etc? And if you are a kinesthetic learner do you use words like: *touch, strike, rub, move, throw,* etc.? Challenge yourself by trying to use words that are not within your learning style. It doesn't take more time out of your day, but it can be one way to stimulate your brain and give it exercise!

My friend, Jerry, was a real visual learner. He had to see everything in order to understand it. One day he decided to challenge himself to other learning styles. Jerry bought a book on tape and started listening to it. Believe it or not, it was hard for him to get the gist of the story. He could remember everything when he watched a movie, but listening without pictures...that was his challenge. Well, Jerry developed that auditory learning, and he now prides himself on this achievement. He is a salesman and travels by car often, so he enjoys all kinds of books on tape.

Children often relate to the kinesthetic style of learning, and sometimes this style is not emphasized in schools. If you have children, have them explore information through all the learning styles. It can motivate them and improve their education.

Stimulating our brains with new information is crucial to the aging process, but we can't just say that all of us should do crossword puzzles or jigsaw puzzles, or learn to play chess. We are each unique, and it depends on our own brain patterns. What we want is to experience new frontiers, learn in different ways, and stimulate our brains so that they don't become dull.

Understand more about your own brain. Explore your potential. Have fun, stay young, and always be enthusiastic in whatever you choose to do!

MY FOUR QUARTERS MENTAL EXERCISE PLAN

MENTAL EXERCISES I WILL DO THAT INCLUDE
LEFT AND RIGHT HEMISPHERES OF THE BRAIN

_____

_____

_____

_____

MY LEARNING STYLE

_____

_____

WHAT I PLAN TO DO TO STIMILATE MY BRAIN

_____

_____

_____

_____

STRESS

Oh! The stress in our lives! If we don't feel stressed, personally, then someone else is telling us how stressed *they* feel. We hear about it on television. We read about it in nearly every magazine we pick up. Stress has become a household word. We can't live with it, and we can't live without it. Stress can occur when your husband won't take you out for that special dinner that he promised, or perhaps your new car broke down, and the warranty won't cover the problem. Maybe you received a call from your daughter's teacher, and she was caught smoking cigarettes on school grounds, or could it be that you went to the doctor's, and you were told that you have a life threatening disease that you now have to cope with. Stress happens when we feel out of control, and it affects every one of us at one time or another. It seems to make sense, don't you think, that if we

143

can't escape it, we might as well learn how to deal with it, or better still, learn to turn it into positive energy that will work for us.

If you're like most people, you experience ups and downs, sometimes feeling anxious, other times feeling happy. In fact, if you took your emotional temperature at different times of the day, it might fluctuate more than you'd expect. A little stress once in a while we barely notice, but too much stress can affect our health. The stress response is controlled by the endocrine system. Our bodies' reaction to stress can vary from increased pupil dilation, perspiration, and increased heart rate and blood pressure, to rapid breathing or muscle tension. Most of us have experienced tension headaches, and many of us have had stomach-aches or insomnia from too much stress. Stress can cause exhaustion and even heart disease or stroke. It can cause loss of sexual desire, aches and pains, missed heartbeats, eating disorders, alcoholism, restlessness, and much more.

Our physical stress comes from lifestyle choices as well as our genetic makeup. If we drink too much coffee or eat too much sugar, we can feel stressed. We can be irritable because we didn't get enough sleep. Most of us have our little "triggers" that set off our own stress responses. I know that if I have too much work to do and not enough time to do it, I feel stressed. These factors are due to lifestyle choices, but genes also have an effect on how stressed we feel. Some of us are just naturally happier than others. We all know people that always seem to have a smile on their face no matter what life throws their way. (Lucky them!) On the other hand, some people take every bump in the road to heart and feel unhappy or stressed over miniscule events. Many people have inherited tendencies towards anxiety disorders or depression. My wife suffered for years off and on with anxiety and panic disorder, as did her father and grandmother, before she overcame it 20 years later. Some of you may be clinically depressed, and you may have other family members who are, as well. There are genetic disorders that cause stress, but whether it is from lifestyle choices or genes, too much stress is unhealthy for us.

There is so much out there that can make us "stressed out": world events, family relations, careers, even little annoyances of the day. Remember how we felt on September 11, 2001? We didn't know how to deal with the terrorists and were afraid to hear the latest news reports. Everyone felt stress. Stress obviously affects our minds in extreme situations, but it can also sneak into our everyday lives over little annoyances. Have you ever misplaced your keys? That can be really stressful, especially if you're in a hurry, but when you think about it, was the stress worth it? Is it *ever* worth it?

From anxiety to control issues, and depression to anger, stress plays a major role in our lives. We can become stressed when someone is rude to us or when we don't get the love we need. Have you ever been to a party where you didn't know anyone? Social events can affect how we feel, too. Some folks would look at this as an opportunity to meet new and interesting people, while many others would feel very uncomfortable in the same situation. What you do for a living can affect your stress level. A lot depends on how much you like your work, of course, as well as how *much* you work. People that find fulfillment in their jobs or careers would probably be less stressed than those who dread the work week.

On the other hand, stress can have positive consequences. If you're stressed because you want to get something done, the stress can motivate you to do it. A lot of people work very efficiently "under the gun." Now, I'm not saying this is the best way to accomplish things, but the stress of not finishing something verses the feeling of satisfaction with a job well done is often just the incentive we need. I know, personally, something as simple as mowing the lawn leaves me feeling stressed if it is not completed. My family thinks I'm in love with mowing because it seems as if I am constantly on my tractor. In reality, if I look out onto my property, and it doesn't look manicured, then I feel stressed!

What it comes down to is this: almost anything can cause stress! We are living in a world that's filled with it, but believe it or not, there are those who just do not succumb to it. They are virtually stress-free! These people know how to control stress. They realize what's important and focus on those things, letting the other less important things just slip by.

How about you? Are you the "everything stresses me out" - type or more the "don't sweat the small stuff" - type of person? Do you feel out of control? Do you want to reduce the stress in your life, and more importantly, do you *need* to reduce your stress for health reasons? If the answer is yes to any of these questions, I have some solutions that will help you change your emotional thermometer so that it doesn't fluctuate quite so much. You *can* be in control of your life, but you have to realize what is important to you—what you need and what you want. This may sound a little philosophical, but let's put some thought into it. Think about the difference between what you *need* and what you *want* out of life. What you *need* are the things that you cannot live without. For example, you can't live without water, air, food, shelter or clothing. What you *want* is everything else! You may want to go out to dinner, but you don't need to go out in order to survive. A 5,000 square foot house would be great, but, of course, you don't need it. You might want to drive a Hummer, but a smaller car would work just as well to get you where you need to be. Every day we make decisions about what is important to us. Some of those decisions are more serious than others, but if you prioritize your needs and think about what is *most* important to you, you may find that you have reduced some of the stress in your life.

THE PROCESS THAT I CAN USE TO REDUCE STRESS

WHAT IS CAUSING MY STRESS? Stop for just a minute, and think about what is causing your stress. Write it down if you can. Be clear about what it is. It doesn't matter whether it is something that others think of as trivial, because if it affects you, it is stressful to you. Some people look at anxiety and stress as a weakness within themselves. If you realize that you are not coping with your life in the way you would like, it doesn't mean that you're weak or that you're incapable of change. It simply means that you are human and dealing with a problem or something that bothers you; so don't beat yourself up over not feeling "like a champion" every day. We all deal with all sorts of problems. The important thing is to recognize that something is bothering you. The problem can be as simple as what dress you should wear to that special occasion or what CD you should buy. Other problems can be a lot more complicated, such as making the decision to begin a course of chemotherapy rather than trying an alternative approach to cancer. You may be frustrated with your co-workers or worried about your child's progress in school. Regardless of whether your problems are simple or complex, once you identify the source of your stress, you can begin to delve into solutions. You may not be able to change the circumstances, but there are ways for you to deal with your stress.

HOW AM I FEELING? Recognize how you are feeling. Think of an emotional thermometer. Are you at a 5 on a scale of 1-10, with 10 being so stressed that you are out of control? Or are you at a 9? It is for you to be aware of how you feel. Don't judge the situation. Think of how you feel about your problem. I have a friend who was just diagnosed with an inoperable melanoma. His stress level is low. He has such a belief in a higher power, that he isn't stressed. I have another friend who was diagnosed with hypertension, and he is so stressed that to him it is the end of the world. You rank your own stress. You can even draw a thermometer and hang it on your refrigerator so that it's in sight for the entire family. I remember when our daughter walked into the house complaining that she and a friend had argued during lunch. I didn't think much of it, but I asked her to think about her emotional thermometer and tell me how important that fight was to her. How did she feel? She said it was a 9 out of 10. I knew at that moment that this was important to her. I sat down and talked with her and asked her what she wanted to do. We figured out a plan, and she resolved the situation.

WHAT DO I WANT? Be concrete and think about a solution that you want. Put on your thinking cap! You know how you feel about the problem. You thought about it in terms of an emotional thermometer. Now it's time to think about the problem. Choose to think it through now, and just for a few minutes, try to let go of your feelings. If the problem is simple, and not life threatening, you may have to think about your values. What is most important to you? Is this problem worth your stress? If it is a complex problem, you may want to think about solutions that are realistic. What's within your control and what isn't? What do you want to do? This is the time to be practical.

WHAT SOLUTIONS CAN HELP ME REDUCE THE STRESS? Now that you know what is stressing you, what the problem actually is, and what solution you would like, congratulate yourself! You have organized some of your thoughts! But that is not enough, because in most cases, you won't get exactly what you want. So brainstorm other solutions to your problem. What can you do to reduce your stress? It doesn't matter whether your problem is extremely simple or extremely complex, you should think of multiple solutions. This is called brainstorming. The better you get at brainstorming and thinking of multiple solutions, the more likely your stress level will be reduced. Remember, it's when we lose control that stress overtakes us. Don't let that happen to you. Have multiple choices, and you will gain control.

WHAT IS MY PLAN? Now it's time to make a plan so that you can reduce that stress. The plan should be something you can actually do, and you might want to include a timeline. Your plan should also include all kinds of goals. Be creative. It should address the problem, but it can also list things just to reduce your stress and the temperature in your emotional thermometer. You can include: going to the movies as a means of distraction from your stress, watching a comedy on TV, or reading a book. Your plan must incorporate practical solutions to deal with your problem. You may need to change your lifestyle to reduce your stress, so your plan should consist of the steps you will take. You may need to include exercise into your weekly routine. When and where will you exercise? Be as specific as possible when you're designing your plan. You may need to ask for help from clergy or a friend. Write down everything you want to accomplish.

Let me share with you a story about my friend, Susan, and how she dealt with a particularly stressful situation. This was a simple problem, so her plan was different than if she had been dealing with a difficult life threatening situation. If Susan did have a complicated problem, though, she could follow the same procedure; however, she would have to analyze the situation and spend more time on her plan. Susan places a lot of emphasis on limiting the stress in her life. She continually thinks what is important to her and what isn't important to her. This has become ingrained in her thinking. She always thinks of a plan.

A few months ago, Susan and her husband, Ron, sat at the breakfast table on a Friday morning. They had just decided to go to their favorite restaurant for dinner that night. Ron was the one who suggested it, and Susan happily agreed. They both went to work, and they both arrived home around 5pm. As soon as Ron walked in the door, he turned to Susan and said, "Let's eat at home instead of going to Nick's. I'm too tired to go."

Feeling angry, Susan said, "So you're changing your mind? I thought we were going to go out for a nice dinner!"

"I don't feel like it," Ron replied, and went upstairs to shower. Susan was upset and disappointed. Her muscles tightened, and she began to sweat. She had the urge to run after Ron and start a fight. How dare him!

What was her problem? The problem was that Susan wanted to go out for a nice dinner, and Ron didn't abide by his original commitment. She was hurt, unhappy, and angry. She had a number of options. She could chase Ron upstairs and demand to go to the restaurant. She could tell him that they needed to talk (although she knew that Ron wasn't in a talking mood), or she could think about what was most important to her.

She chose the latter. She wrote down five things she wanted right then and there.

1. A good dinner at Nick's
2. A nice relaxing evening
3. A healthy relationship with Ron
4. A beginning to a good weekend
5. An understanding from Ron that he hurt her

She prioritized her list and recognized that numbers 3 and 5 were most important to her. Dinner at Nick's wasn't at the top of the list. She valued her relationship with Ron more than a night out. So she thought of a number of things she could do and decided to run to the closest Chinese restaurant, pick up two orders of chow mien, rush home, set the table with china dishes, and light candles. She did all of that, and by the time Ron came downstairs, the music was playing, and the atmosphere was relaxed and peaceful.

During dinner Ron said, "Why did you do this?" Susan explained that the relationship was more important to her than the dinner out. At which time Ron said, "I'm sorry that I hurt you" — the exact words that Susan needed to hear. Ron proceeded to tell Susan that his deal had fallen through at work, and he wasn't feeling like a dinner out where they would see their friends and where he'd have to put on a happy face. Yet, he hadn't worked through all of that when he walked in the front door. When he said, "I don't feel like going out to dinner. I'm tired," he was preoccupied with his own situation and hadn't meant to disappoint his wife.

Susan made a choice. We all do, in every situation that surrounds us. We, as human beings, are like a computer with a million different web sites. If we turn on the web site to thoughtfulness, we become thoughtful. If we turn on the web site to anger, we become angry. We have to take each situation and think: what is most important to me? What do I value? Go with those things in life that hold meaning to you.

I CAN REDUCE MY STRESS

Check at least five stress reducers that you will use on a daily basis.
1. Try to look at the positive things happening in your life. Think about what you can change to become more positive and less negative.
2. Prioritize your needs and your wants. Think about what is most important to you and focus on it. Go with your heart, not your ego.
3. Ask yourself, "How important will this be for me next week? Next month? Next year?" Put the stress in perspective. Don't put more importance on something than it deserves
4. Call a friend. Talking about what is bothering you, often minimizes the problem.
5. Go out and take a walk, listen to music, or tell jokes.
6. Go to a movie, and just have fun for a few hours.
7. Focus on your breathing. You will notice that when you are extremely stressed, your breathing becomes uneven. If you close your eyes and just focus on your breath for five minutes, you will feel more relaxed.

8. Keep a journal of your stresses. Find patterns in what makes you stressed. Make changes in your thinking and your actions.
9. Take mini breaks when you get stressed at work.
10. Don't sweat the small stuff!
11. Laugh
12. Dance
13. Visualize yourself in a positive way. Negative visualization will produce negative results. Positive visualization will produce positive results. Visualize your life the way you want it to be!
14. Do away with negative words. Eliminate the words: SHOULD, BUT, HOWEVER, IMPOSSIBLE, CAN'T, and DIFFICULT.
15. If you want to change your life——TAKE ACTION. Be positive. Change is only possible when you take control. No one can change you but you!
16. Surround yourself with people who have a positive attitude. When you choose to be around people who are often angry and negative, it is easier for you to become that way. The opposite is true as well. When you stick with positive people, you become that way!
17. Take responsibility for your own mood and attitude. Don't let others influence you.
18. Speak in a direct manner, but show respect to your co-workers. Try not to "beat around the bush".
19. If you are doing most of the talking, then think twice. Ask questions. Bring out the best in yourself and others. Conversations are 50-50!
20. SMILE! Smile at yourself in the mirror, smile at other people. Smile whenever you think of it. Smiling will automatically make you feel a little (or a lot) happier. Do it often!
21. Reduce stress by stretching, using a squeeze ball or receiving a massage.
22. You can't always change your circumstances, but YOU CAN CHANGE YOUR ATTITUDE. You choose how you REACT to things.
23. Close your eyes. Focus on your breathing. Count each breath up to ten. Slowly open your eyes, stretch your arms and shoulders, and smile!
24. Visualize one of the following: the color red, the screech of chalk on a chalkboard, the slamming of brakes. Now think of where the ten-

sion lies in your body. Relax by making the color red fade into a light soft blue, the screech of chalk turn into the sound of your favorite singer, the slamming of brakes into someone giving you a rub down.

25. Make extra time: Cut down on television, limit phone conversations, get up an hour earlier two times a week, take a shorter shower.

26. Learn to say "NO". If you have too much to do, you might be the kind of person who doesn't know how to say no. Set priorities. If someone asks you to do something, think first.

27. Set reasonable goals. You can't do it all!

28. Focus on the process, not the end result. When you enjoy the process, you actually get the task done more quickly.

29. Make lists. Sound like a waste of time? I guarantee that it will add time. Make the list in the morning, and check off the items throughout the day.

30. Believe in yourself.

SIGNS OF STRESS

- anger
- fatigue
- weight gain or loss
- irritability
- poor memory
- pain
- muscle tension
- fear
- poor relationships
- anxiety
- heart palpitations
- twitching
- nervous tension

WHAT PRODUCES THE STRESS IN ME?

- genes
- self-esteem
- lifestyle
- country/world events
- environment
- chemical imbalance in the body
- job demands
- lack of decision making skills
- health
- finances

MY FOUR QUARTERS PLAN TO REDUCE STRESS

1. WHAT IS MY PROBLEM?_____
_____
_____

2. WHAT TRIGGERS THE STRESS IN MY LIFE?
_____
_____
_____

3. WHAT ARE MY FEELINGS?
_____
_____
_____

4. WHAT DO I WANT?
_____
_____
_____

5. WHAT STRESS REDUCERS WORK FOR ME?
_____
_____
_____

6. GIVE MULTIPLE SOLUTIONS
_____
_____
_____

7. WHAT IS MY PLAN?
_____
_____
_____

SLEEP

GET A GOOD NIGHT'S SLEEP!
SLEEP FACTS & REMEDIES

- You're not the only one awake! Sleep (or lack of it) is a major problem for millions of Americans. There are many remedies, though, to get a good night's sleep. Start with a bedtime routine. Go to bed at the same time every night, seven nights a week. Yes, that means weekends and days off too!

- You may think that if you lose one hour of sleep a night, it won't hurt you. WRONG. If you lose one hour of sleep a night for seven nights, it's as if you lost a whole night's sleep. It all adds up.

- Don't think that you will catch up on your sleep on weekends. You need to stick to a regular schedule. If you lose sleep, you are tired during the day.

- Be careful not to become dependent on sleeping pills. Before you take them, talk with your doctor. LOOK at the labels. Never take more than the recommended dose. Don't stay on them for longer than the recommended time. You may want to try taking less than the recommended dose. Some may leave you feeling groggy the next day. Most people can get a good night's sleep if they follow a healthy lifestyle and maintain a bedtime routine. Eliminate those pills!

- Be aware that over-the-counter medication like antihistamines can make you tired and groggy. Read the labels.

- Stop driving if you are tired. Adjust the temperature in your vehicle. Don't make it too warm. Heat will make you even more sleepy.

- SLEEP APNEA occurs when a person temporarily stops breathing while he/she is sleeping. Most people with sleep apnea are not diagnosed with it, yet it is a dangerous disease. Don't take it lightly. If someone tells you that you stopped breathing or you were gasping for breath when you were asleep, call your doctor and get help. It can be treated successfully.

- Don't consume caffeine for several hours before bed. It can make it difficult for you to fall asleep.

- Alcohol can disturb your sleeping patterns. It may seem to relax you, but the relaxation doesn't follow you throughout the night.

- Signs of fatigue: Heavy eyelids, eyes that can't focus, excessive yawning, confused thoughts, problems remembering.

- FACT: The National Highway Safety Administration estimates that at least 100,000 crashes, 71,000 injuries, and 1500 fatalities occur each year caused by drivers who fall asleep at the wheel. Stay alert on the road. Watch out for the other drivers too! You need to be quick enough to get out of their way!

- Exercise early in the day to get a good night's sleep. Don't exercise right before bed. It will stimulate you and keep you awake.

- Take 30 minutes before bed to relax. Read a book, watch a funny TV program, or listen to your favorite music.

- Eat light at night. If you must have a snack before bed, try a bowl of cereal, a graham cracker and glass of milk, a piece of fruit, or yogurt.

GET 6-8 HOURS OF SLEEP A NIGHT

Answer the following:

Are you content with the amount of sleep you get?

_____

How do you feel when you are tired?

_____

How do you treat others when you are tired?

_____

How do you cope with sleep deprivation _____

_____

_____

Is your bedroom conducive to sleep?_____

Is your productivity affected when you don't get enough sleep?

_____

Do you have less energy when you don't get enough sleep?

_____

What is your mood when you are sleep deprived?

_____

Do you become angry, stressed out, lethargic, and unable to cope with ordinary circumstances when you are tired?

_____

Do you lack concentration when you are tired?

_____

Can you think logically and make decisions when you are tired?

_____

What are some of the effects you feel when you lack sleep?

_____

_____

_____

MY FOUR QUARTERS PLAN FOR SLEEP

WHAT INFORMATION DO I NEED IN ORDER TO BE INFORMED ABOUT MY SLEEP HABITS?

_____

_____

_____

DO I HAVE A POSITIVE ATTITUDE ABOUT THE SLEEP I NEED?

_____

_____

AM I COMMITTED TO GETTING AT LEAST 6-8 HOURS OF SLEEP A NIGHT?

_____

_____

_____

DO I HAVE A PLAN SO THAT I CAN GET THE SLEEP I NEED?

_____

_____

_____

WHAT IS MY BEDTIME ROUTINE?_____

_____

_____

HOW DO I NEED TO ADJUST MY SCHEDULE?

_____

_____

_____

Month _____

1	2	3	4	5	6	7
8	9	10	11	12	13	14
15	16	17	18	19	20	21
22	23	24	25	26	27	28
29	30	31				

ATTITUDE AND HAPPINESS

Everyone wants to have a positive attitude towards life and be happy. I haven't met anyone who has said, "I'd rather be miserable!" But many of us don't know how to get to that happy state of mind. We wake up in the morning and plug through the day. We complain about the hardships in life and wish things could be different.

I am going to tell you that things can be different. You don't have to be miserable, and you can reach a state of satisfaction and happiness...something that many people don't know how to achieve.

I will take you through ten steps. Each will get you closer to that 'happy state of mind,' but it is up to you to follow the steps. You know the expression, "You can lead a horse to water, but you can't make him drink." I can lead you on the road, but it is ultimately your choice to follow it.

MY FOUR QUARTERS PLAN TO A HEALTHY ATTITUDE AND HAPPINESS

STEP ONE

Think about your life NOW.

Do you accept and love yourself?	Yes	No
Do you feel in control of your life?	Yes	No
Do you look at the glass as 'half full' and not 'half empty'?	Yes	No
Do you get up in the morning filled with excitement?	Yes	No
Do you take good care of yourself?	Yes	No
Do you know your purpose in life?	Yes	No
Do you avoid worrying too much?	Yes	No
Do you know how to enjoy yourself?	Yes	No
Do you avoid negative situations?	Yes	No
Do you easily forgive others?	Yes	No

Out of a possible 10 points, what was your score? If you answered yes to all 10 questions, then you can most likely skip this section. But if you have a score of less than 7, which is typical of most of us, READ on!

STEP TWO

Accept yourself! If you don't, no one else will! It's okay to make mistakes. It's okay to not be first. It's okay to be worthy of love. You may have been taught that you aren't okay. You are too fat...too thin...not smart enough...not rich enough...not good enough...and so on. Don't let others challenge the love that you deserve. You deserve love just because you are a human being. You deserve for others to treat you with respect, and they will...if you accept yourself. Stop the blame game! You have the right to feel the way you do. You have the right to be who you are. Start today with the acceptance of yourself. Every time you put yourself down, either verbally or to yourself, turn it around and say to yourself, "I am okay. I am the best I can be at this time."

STEP THREE

Consider what your life might be if you valued yourself *all* the time. Your thoughts reflect who you are, but you have to recognize those positive thoughts and be proud of them. Some of them are conscious while others are subconscious, and they've been formed over all the years of your life. The more time you focus on the positive thoughts, the less time you will think of the negative ones. The more times you are in touch with those positive thoughts, the happier you will be.

Take out a small piece of paper. List five positive thoughts you have about yourself. You might say: I am sensitive toward others. I get things done. I am filled with energy. I listen when others speak.

1. _____
2. _____
3. _____
4. _____
5. _____

List three more positive thoughts.

6. _____
7. _____
8. _____

Today, focus on those positive thoughts. Any time a situation occurs in which you feel out of control, go to that small piece of paper and think of your positive qualities. One of them will help you deal with the situation at hand.

STEP FOUR

It's time to think about what you value most in life. In the space below, put the five most important things in your life. You can list your family, your friends, your work, your church, anything that matters the most to you. Family can be one of the five, or you can break it down to include each member. There are no rules to follow.

1. _____
2. _____
3. _____
4. _____
5. _____

Now I would like you to cross out two things so that you have only three left. Can you cross out another one? Can you choose the *one* most important thing in your life? Think about what you value the most. Do you live by what you value?

For example, if you say that your family is the most important thing in your life, do you spend enough time with them? If you don't, you probably are unhappy and confused. It is a normal feeling, because you aren't following your heart. Start readjusting your life so that you live by your values. You can't change your values, because what you value is so deep set within you. Your only choice is to rethink your lifestyle and accommodate that which is most important to you.

STEP FIVE

We all have a purpose in life. Without realizing your purpose, life can be unfulfilling. Your purpose doesn't have to be overwhelming. You don't have to save the world, but you have to know your purpose. It takes some thinking. I will bring you through the process.

First, consider those things that you do with your time. Write down the major things that you do. Include your work and your free time activities.

_____
_____
_____
_____

Second, think about all those things that you would love to do. Let your mind wander. Don't dismiss any idea. Just go with the flow. This is the time to daydream. Out of daydreams and wishes come direction.

Write those dreams and wishes

_____

_____

Third, think about your values. How do they fit into the things you do and those things you would love to do? Give some thought to their relationship.

Fourth, it's time to take action. You know the activities you do, those that you love to do, and your values. How can you combine them all? This will lead you toward your life's purpose. Go for it!

My Life's Purpose is _____

_____

_____

_____

Don't think that your life's purpose has to stay the same forever. It doesn't. You have to continually go back to the drawing board. Your kids can grow up and leave the house. You can have grandchildren that you want to take care of. You can have a job that you love and that fills all of your time. Just make sure that what you do fulfills your values, the activities that you presently do, and your dreams!

STEP SIX

In order to have a good attitude and to be happy, it is important to avoid as many negative situations as you can. Sometimes that is impossible to do. If you have a nagging mother-in-law, but you love your spouse, you can't always stay away from your mother-in-law.

There are things, though, that you can control. In fact, you probably choose most of your situations. Don't spend time in negative situations that make you feel powerless. If you work in an office and there is too much office gossip, recognize that you can choose to walk away from it. Go outside for lunch, get some fresh air, walk away from trouble, surround yourself by those who make you feel happy and feel good about yourself.

How much time do you spend with people who are unhappy or people that put you down? If you're around people who take your energy away from you rather than give it to you, then you are making yourself unhappy. Surround yourself with positive feelings, positive thoughts, and positive people.

What negative situations do you need to eliminate or at least reduce?_____
_____
_____
_____

What positive situations do you need to increase?
_____
_____
_____
_____

STEP SEVEN

What do you need to change about yourself? You named those positive feelings you have about yourself, but what is it that you need to change? I know that I used to get angry at myself when I didn't get everything done at the office. I needed to change my expectations. It was hard for me at first, but I thought about what I value most. The answer for me is my family. If I stayed at the office too long so that I could finish my list of things I wanted to do, it took time away from my wife and children. For awhile, I rationalized and said that I was making money and working for my wife and kids. Sure, that is true, but in reality, I wasn't spending time with them, and therefore I was hurting myself. I forced myself to leave the office in time to pick up Erica at school. I realized that I was happier on the days I picked her up and not as happy on the days that I stayed at the office.

STEP EIGHT

Stop Worrying! We worry about so many things in our lives, but over 90% of our worries don't ever come to fruition. We worry about not having enough money. We worry about not having a job next year. We worry about house payments. We worry about gaining too much weight. We worry about getting cancer. We worry about having a heart attack. And so on.

How much do you worry? Make a worry list. Put down everything that worries you. Don't eliminate anything. Fold the paper so that you have two columns next to your worry list. The first says WORRY CAME TRUE and the second says, I WAS WRONG! Now, hang your worry list on the refrigerator. Look at it daily. How often do you have to place a mark next to the WORRY CAME TRUE statement? I bet it is far less often than the I WAS WRONG statements. Every time you worry about something, think of your worry list.

How can you worry less? A simple way to reduce your worries is to live one day at a time. Think about what you can do THIS day to make it the best it can be for you. Don't let things out of your control take over. YOU control your day. If you have a difficult time with one day at a time, think about one hour at a time.

When you live in the present, you'll find that you worry less and enjoy your days. Sometimes it may seem hard to let go of your worries. You turn on the TV and you hear, 'Save now for your retirement. Do you have money to pay for your funeral? Are you planning for your children's college education?' Those are some of the questions we hear in commercials, from financial planners, and from insurance brokers. No doubt, we must think ahead. But we must have a balance in our lives and take one day at a time. What do I mean by that? I mean that you must prepare for the future, but live in the present. If you don't enjoy the day, you are missing out on your life. Try to reduce that worry list and live one day at a time.

STEP NINE

FORGIVING AND NOT JUDGING OTHERS

Practice forgiveness, and you will feel better about yourself. If you hold onto a grudge, it only hurts you. If you are angry with someone, it eats away at you. If you blame others...judge others, it only causes you unhappiness. Without forgiveness, happiness cannot exist.

Most of us have had a relative that has made us angry. That is, really angry! I know that I have. Think about someone in your family who has given you problems. How are you dealing with your anger? Can you forgive that person? I believe that we learn the most from our families. Our most difficult lessons often come from our relatives. You've heard the expression, "You can choose your friends, but you can't choose your relatives." The statement is true, but as long as you hold that anger, and don't forgive, it only hurts you.

Your attitude will change if you stop judging others. Sometimes we make judgments that are not based on all of the information we need. If you start to judge someone, think about this situation.

My friend, Jeffrey, recently learned a lot about judgment. He was in New York City for a conference that lasted two weeks. On Sunday, he decided to go to a museum and took the subway. He walked onto the subway and sat down with his New York Times. He was content. He was reading the Book Review section, sipping his espresso and feel-

168

ing good about the day. A grubby looking man with his three dirty children walked on and sat down next to Jeffrey. His children ran up and down the subway. They were so annoying!. He kept quiet, trying to read his paper, but eventually he thought, 'I am going to give this guy a piece of my mind. What right does he have allowing his kids to disturb everyone here? He's a real bum.' So Jeffrey turned to the man and said, "Could you please get your kids under control. They're disturbing everyone." To which the man replied, "Oh, sir. I am so sorry. I didn't even realize it. You see, we are coming home from spending the night at the hospital. My wife (and their mother) just died." Jeffrey felt awful. He never imagined that this man was dirty and his kids were running around because of those circumstances. He made assumptions that were totally wrong. Don't judge others, because you don't know their entire story. None of us can know exactly how someone else feels, what they are thinking, and what their experiences were to lead up to their behavior.

STEP TEN

TYING IT ALL TOGETHER

Take time to review these steps and decide which ones you need to work on the most. Keep at it! Keeping a positive attitude is a life-long process. Being happy is within your reach.

Describe yourself

_____
_____
_____

Accept yourself! Name two ways you will do it.

_____
_____
_____
_____

What are those positive feelings that you will focus on today?

_____

_____

_____

_____

What are your values?

_____

_____

_____

_____

What negative situations will you avoid today?

_____

_____

_____

_____

What is your life's purpose? Be specific.

_____

_____

_____

_____

What do you want to change about yourself and how will you do it?

_____

_____

_____

_____

Write out your worry list. Focus on reducing it.

WORRY CAME TRUE   **I WAS WRONG!**

_____
_____
_____
_____
_____
_____
_____
_____
_____
_____

Who do you intend to forgive and how will you go about doing it?

_____
_____
_____
_____
_____

How do you intend to stop judging others?

_____
_____
_____
_____

BEHAVIOR HURDLE NUMBER ONE

TIME MANAGEMENT

MY FOUR QUARTERS PLAN TO MANAGE MY TIME

Do you have problems managing your time? Is it difficult to get everything done that you want to do? Do you try to fit an exercise program into your life, but you are unsuccessful? There just aren't enough hours in the day. Follow this process and I guarantee that you will find that you have more time than you ever realized.

Think of an activity that you would like to include in your life. Write it down and include the reason why you want to do it.

_____

_____

_____

_____

_____

_____

Think about the days of the week that you want to do this activity. It can be one day or seven days. Circle those days.

Sunday   Monday   Tuesday

Wednesday   Thursday   Friday

Saturday

What are your best hours to do this activity? How do you feel at each of these times?

8am_____
9am_____
10am_____
11am_____
12pm_____
1pm_____
2pm_____
3pm_____
4pm_____
5pm_____
6pm_____
7pm_____
8pm_____
9pm_____
10pm_____
11pm_____
12pm_____
1am_____
2am_____
3am_____
4am_____
5am_____
6am_____
7am_____

Many of you may say, "But I still don't have the time." Just keep going with this plan. You will find that you really do have time for this activity. For the next week follow this time management plan. It just may change your thinking! It may just change your life!

STEP ONE

Think of all those things you have to do and want to do today. Write them down.

Here's an example of a To-Do list:

To Do
Look for a new car
Give the dog a bath
Eat a large, healthy bowl of granola for breakfast
Drive to work
Go to the gym
Read the newspaper
Relax before bed
Go to the bank
Go to the library because I am almost finished with this novel
Wash my car
Call the travel agent
Watch television.

MY TO-DO LIST

_____ ( )
_____ ( )
_____ ( )
_____ ( )
_____ ( )
_____ ( )
_____ ( )
_____ ( )
_____ ( )
_____ ( )
_____ ( )
_____ ( )

STEP TWO

Think about prioritizing your list.
What's important and what's NOT...
Let's look at the sample list and prioritize it.
Then prioritize your own list, above

Place #1 next to those items you must do.
Place #2 next to those items that are very important.
Place #3 next to those items that can wait.

Eat a large, healthy breakfast ....(1)
Drive to work ....(1)
Go to the gym ....(1)
Read the newspaper ....(1)
Relax before bed ....(1)
Look for a new car..(2)
Go to the bank..(2)
Go to the library and get new books to read ....(2)
Wash my car...(3)
Call my mother-in-law...(3)
Give the dog a bath ....(3)
Watch television...(3)

STEP THREE

There are some things in life that you MUST do, others that you want to do. If the doctor told you that you would die in three months if you didn't exercise one hour a day or if you didn't start eating more fruits and vegetables, chances are you would start doing both. It is essential for you to know what is important for you to do and what isn't as vital.

Let's go one step further. Think about the same list, but let's look at six objectives.

Number #1...Most important——MUST DO.
Number #2...Important, but not as important as Number 1.
Number #3...Want to do- but may have to eliminate
Number #4...Don't want to do, but MUST DO.
Number #5...Don't want to do and don't have to do.

Let's look at the same sample list. How has it changed?

		Step Two's List
Eat a large, healthy breakfast	(2)	(1)
Drive to work	(1)	(1)
Go to the gym	(2)	(1)
Read the nespaper	(3)	(1)
Relax before bed	(3)	(1)
Look for a new car	(3)	(2)
Go to the bank	(2)	(2)
Go to the library and get new books to read.	(3)	(2)
Wash my car	(3)	(3)
Call my mother-in-law	(4)	(3)
Give the dog a bath	(3)	(3)
Watch television	(3)	(3)

MY TO-DO LIST

_____ ( )

_____ ( )

_____ ( )

_____ ( )

_____ ( )

_____ ( )

_____ ( )

_____ ( )

_____ ( )

_____ ( )

_____ ( )

_____ ( )

What are your REAL priorities?

STEP FOUR

YOUR SCHEDULE...

If you want to change your lifestyle, you must place the change you want to make as Number 1, or Number 4. (Most important...MUST DO or Don't want to do, but MUST DO) Then, PLAN to do it. BUT it also must fit into your lifestyle.

Look at *your* TO-DO list. Place the change you want to make on your TO-DO list.

Let's say you haven't been exercising and would like to add an hour long workout into your daily routine. There are more factors than a TO-DO List to consider, such as the following:

Am I a night person?
Am I a morning person?
Do I like a full schedule?
Do I need alone time?
Do I need more time management skills?
Do I need to get organized?

Think about how these questions relate to your goal.

For instance, if you are a night person, then exercising in the late afternoon might be best for you. If you are a morning person, then you might decide that you can get up an hour early, and walk before your day begins. If you like a full schedule, then you probably can squeeze the hour of exercise into your present routine, but if you like time alone and don't like to be busy every second, you may need to eliminate some of those things that can wait.

How do you deal with those things that are MOST IMPORTANT to you? How will you make sure to get them done?

_____ ( )
_____ ( )
_____ ( )
_____ ( )
_____ ( )

STEP FIVE

The more you understand about yourself: what you want to do, and why you want to do it, the more easily you will meet your goal. Let's take the example of developing an exercise program. Think about the reasons you want to exercise. (This can apply to anything that you want to add into your life.)

Why do you want to improve your health?

_____

_____

_____

What is your chance for success? When you start an activity, you've already decided whether you will succeed at it or not. You already have most of the answers; you just may not recognize them. Answer the following questions.

	(low) -1	2	3	4	(high) 5
I have the ability to do this activity.					
I have the time to include this activity in my schedule.					
I want to do this activity.					
I need to do this activity.					

Based on your answers, do you think you will succeed? _____

_____

_____

DON'T STOP TRYING! If you don't succeed, then try, and try, and *try* again!

Think about this man who just didn't give up! Who is he? He lost his job early in his career. He tried to run for a political position, but he lost the election. He started a business, but failed. He had a nervous breakdown. He ran for another political position, but lost that election too. He waited a few years, then ran for Speaker of the House and lost. He tried to become a land officer but he was rejected. He didn't give up. He decided to run for another political position, but he LOST again! He still didn't give up! He ran for US Senate and LOST again. He ran for Vice President of the United States and . . . LOST AGAIN.

He was Abraham Lincoln! What lessons can we learn from him? Succeeding in something means trying over and over again. You may not succeed on your first attempt. Most of us don't, but it is only those who give up, that never succeed. It isn't easy to add something into your busy schedule. It has to become a habit, and that takes time and persistence. Don't give up and this activity will become a habit for you.

It's time to think through your plan:

1. Activity I want to do _____

_____

_____

_____

2. Two reasons I want to do this activity _____

_____

_____

_____

3. What is my chance of success? _____

_____

_____

_____

4. Do I feel I can handle the commitment to it? _____

_____

_____

5. Am I willing to try... and if I fail...try, try and try again? _____

_____

_____

_____

6. Am I committed to doing something for myself? _____

_____

_____

_____

7. What is your goal?

Long-term goal

_____

_____

Short-term goal (for next week)

_____

_____

_____

BEHAVIOR HURDLE NUMBER TWO

MOTIVATION

Sometimes it seems impossible to get motivated. You look at other people and they seem so together. They go to the gym. They get things done on time. They don't procrastinate. They make a decision and stick to it. It seems so easy for them. And for you? No way. Does this sound familiar? "For New Year's, I am joining the gym. I am going to work out five days a week." "I am going on a diet. I know it is my hundredth time, but this time it will work." But again, it doesn't!

So what makes some people motivated? Are they born that way? Do they have some special gift that you don't have? NO–and that is an emphatic NO! You can do it just like them. You can get motivated and stay motivated.

You need to learn how to change your behavior just like you learn how to do anything new. If you take up a new hobby, let's say chess, you don't just become a good chess player by willing it. You have to learn how to play the game; you have to stay motivated and play over and over again. You have to constantly think about the rules of the game. There are many things you have to do in order to become a good chess player.

What about sports? Let's say you want to get your black belt in Karate. You can't walk into a studio and say, "I would like a black belt today!" You have to earn it. How do you go about earning it? My friend, Jen, can tell you. She started out as a white belt. She had to learn her forms, or katas. There were three forms, Kipon one, two and three. She went to class three times a week for two months. Then she had to go on a Saturday morning and take a test along with fifty other students. She passed and became a yellow belt. She stayed at that level for about six months and finally moved on to a green belt. She worked at her forms. She continued to go to class three times a week. After three years, she finally became a brown belt. She was so proud of herself! With much perseverance, two years later, she took her black belt test. SHE PASSED! What an achievement.

What motivated Jen? She wasn't an athlete, but Jen decided that she needed to do some form of exercise. She had gained weight over the years. Her blood pressure was too high, and the doctor wanted to put her on medication if she didn't lower it within six months. The doctor told her that she could have a stroke. Her mother died of a stroke at age 56. Jen was 53. Just last year, her sister had a minor stroke, so there was a good chance that Jen could have severe consequences. Jen went through this process that I am going to take you through, and she lowered her blood pressure and lost weight. She got motivated. So can you!

Let's begin. What do you want to change?

_____

_____

On a scale from 1-10, how important is it for you <u>physically</u> to make this change?
(Not at all) 1   2   3   4   5   6   7   8   9   10 (will do everything possible)

On a scale from 1-10, how important is it for you <u>emotionally</u> to make this change?
(Not at all) 1   2   3   4   5   6   7   8   9   10 (will do everything possible)

On a scale from 1-10, will something bad happen to you if you don't make this change?
(Not at all) 1   2   3   4   5   6   7   8   9   10 (YES!)

If your answers are close to a 10 on all three questions, chances are you will succeed, but still may need help getting motivated. If your answers are much lower than 10, your level of motivation is probably fairly low. Don't dismay! You can also succeed. Go for it! Start with STEP ONE.

MY FOUR QUARTERS PLAN TOWARD MOTIVATION

STEP ONE

The first step in this process is to think about your self esteem. Your self-esteem affects your level of motivation. If you feel loved and appreciated, you will be more likely to want to do positive things for yourself. The reverse is also true. If you feel unappreciated and feel you have no sense of power, your level of motivation decreases. This doesn't mean you can't do anything about it. YOU CAN. First you must be aware of yourself. Look at the list below, and answer the questions based on how you feel about yourself. Go back over the list, and circle those things that you would like to change. Then think about how you can change them. Sometimes it is asking for something that you need. For example, if you do all of the housework, and your spouse or partner does nothing, yet all you want is appreciation——ask for it! "I need for you to notice that I vacuumed, dusted, shopped, took the kids for new shoes, and made dinner for everyone." A little thanks goes a long way.

	Little									Great
	1	2	3	4	5	6	7	8	9	10

I have power at home

I have power at work

Most people appreciate me

I feel self confident

I feel loved

I feel valued

I am an exceptional person

I know I can accomplish a lot in life

I know my life's purpose

I feel motivated to stay healthy

I accept challenges

I feel worthwhile

I hold myself accountable for what I do

I have a positive self image

I am able to make decisions

I feel successful

Think about how these factors relate to your level of motivation. For example, if you don't feel success in your work or personal life, how do you think it affects the change you want to make? How can you change some of the negative feelings about yourself to positive ones?

My suggestion is to change your thinking. You can't always change your circumstances, <u>but you can change your thinking</u>. If you think positive thoughts about yourself, you will tend to get positive results. Try it. You may just like what you see!

STEP TWO

How you respond to life situations affects your level of motivation. For example, if you usually take responsibility for your own health, you will more likely succeed at changes that involve health related issues. You will lose weight, exercise, and learn different stress techniques. Look at the statements below and decide which ones are important to you based on that one change you want to make.

Put a T for True next to those statements that describe you...and an F for False for those that do not. Think about your answers in relation to your motivation.

1. I know what my life's purpose is.

2. I choose my lifestyle.

3. I take responsibility for my own health.

4. I go to the doctor prepared with questions.

5. I am able to control my moods.

6. I accept change in my life.

7. I make time to do what I think is important.

8. I am well respected in my community.

9. I sometimes do things that I don't like to do, but know that they are good for me.

10. I choose to be surrounded by positive people.

11. I think before I speak.

12. I know how to relax.

13. I value the opinion of others, but listen to my own intuition.

14. I keep physically active.

15. I don't let others control me.

16. I have a positive attitude about life.

17. I am an optimist.

18. I keep stress to a minimum.

19 I am organized.

20. I am loveable.

How do your answers relate to the change you want to make? _____

_____

_____

_____

STEP THREE

Your values affect your level of motivation. Choose five items below that are important to you. Put them in order of importance. One is the most important.

VALUES

Be in good shape

Have close relationships

Be self-sufficient

Have a nice home

Have a strong religious faith

Be financially secure

Have a stimulating job

Be peaceful

Be healthy

Be physically attractive

Be involved in the community

Be prosperous

Be physically active

Have a tight-knit family life

Be well-respected

Be in love

Be gifted

What I value the most:

1. _____

2. _____

3. _____

4. _____

5. _____

Write a few sentences about your values and the connection you see to your level of motivation.

STEP FOUR

Knowing how to break old habits raises your level of motivation. If you are happy with your life, and you are happy with all of your habits, that's great! But most of us want to improve our lifestyles. We want to wake up in the morning refreshed and happy. We want, we want, we want... We don't always get what we want, because we just don't know how to break those old habits.

To get what you want, you must accept who you are right now. It doesn't mean that you can't make change. It doesn't mean that you are fulfilled right now. It means that you recognize that you can't change what already has happened, but you can change what you do from now on. You can not change the past, but you can change a lot about the future. You can change your habits.

Breaking old patterns is possible, but you have to know what you can change. Think about The Serenity Prayer and what changes you have the courage to make and what things you cannot change.

God grant me the
Serenity to accept the things I cannot change,
The courage to change the things I can,
And the wisdom to know the difference.

Things I cannot change

_____

_____

_____

Things I can change

_____

_____

_____

Things I have the courage to change

_____

_____

_____

Reasons I want to make this change.

_____

_____

_____

What I will lose if I don't make the change.

_____

_____

_____

The most important thing I must do to make this change

_____

_____

_____

STEP FIVE

Knowing how to make change raises your level of motivation. We have gone through this process in the Nutrition section, but it can help you with any change. I am repeating this section intentionally so that you can reinforce it. The first story is about Joe, a man who wants to get into an exercise program. The second story is about Kathleen, who wants to lose weight. Focus on the process that they both have to go through in order to accomplish their goal.

JOE...

"I can't do it....its too hard... I've tried a million times to develop an exercise routine, and I end up getting nowhere." Look at the process that Joe must go through to include exercise into his daily routine. This is what he has to ask himself.

WHAT IS MY SITUATION? Joe has to be aware of his problem. He must recognize that he is at risk for heart disease if he doesn't strengthen his heart. His father died of a heart attack at age 39. Joe is 37, and the doctor told him that he may need heart surgery. Joe is aware of the danger, so he moves on to his goal.

WHAT ARE MY GOALS? "I need to develop an aerobic exercise program that will improve my cardiovascular fitness. I need to walk a 15 minute mile with ease." Once Joe recognizes his goal, then he thinks about why he wants to change.

WHY DO I NEED TO CHANGE? Joe says, "I want to live to a ripe old age, unlike my father. I want to be around for my kids, so I know I must start a walking program." If he REALLY wants to start a regular walking routine, then he needs certain information.

WHAT INFORMATION DO I NEED? Knowledge is power. Joe needs to have facts about aerobic exercise; what he can do and what he can't do...and he also needs to know certain specific information- such as his target heart rate. He has to obtain the information, whether it is on the Internet, at a bookstore, or at the library. If he thoroughly researches the information, then he looks at the benefits that this change will have for him.

WHAT BENEFITS WILL I RECEIVE IF I CHANGE? Joe needs to recognize the benefits he will get if he starts walking regularly. If he doesn't look at exercise as something negative, but realizes what he will gain (reduction in stress, lower blood pressure, etc), then he ponders the problems that arise.

WHAT PROBLEMS MAY ARISE? Joe has to think about the problems he might face. "Do I have the time to exercise? I may need a mini course in time management. What if it rains? I hate being outside in the cold." If he knows how to successfully deal with these problems, change becomes less difficult.

Now let's look at KATHLEEN...

"I can't do it....its too hard... I've tried a million times and I fail." IT'S NOT TOO LATE to make change. Look at the chart below to understand the process that a young woman, Kathleen, must go through to make change in her eating habits. This is what she has to ask herself.

WHAT IS MY SITUATION? Kathleen has to be aware of her problem. She must recognize that she is eating too much food. If she knows that she eats too much, then she thinks about her goal.

WHAT ARE MY GOALS?. "I need to lose weight. I need to reduce the number of calories I am eating. I am already 25 pounds overweight." Once Kathleen recognizes her goal, then she has to start thinking about why she wants to change. She has to have a reason that is very important to her.

WHY SHOULD I CHANGE? Kathleen says, "I want to lose 25 pounds. I don't want to get diabetes like my mother and sister." If she REALLY wants to lose 25 pounds, then she tries to figure out the information she needs.

WHAT INFORMATION DO I NEED? Knowledge is power. Kathleen needs to know how many calories she is eating every day. She can call a nutritionist, go to the library, take a course on nutrition, or go to the bookstore and find those books that relate to the information she needs. If she thoroughly researches the information, then she is ready to think about the benefits she will get if she does follow through with her goal.

WHAT BENEFITS WILL I RECEIVE IF I CHANGE? Kathleen needs to recognize the benefits she will get if she starts counting calories. If she knows that this is the best way for her to lose weight, and she is willing to start counting calories, then she addresses the problems that may arise.

WHAT PROBLEMS MAY ARISE? Kathleen has to think about the problems she might face. "Does my husband really like me overweight? If I don't have snack foods, etc. around the house, will the kids nag me? Will I continue to count calories after two weeks?" If she knows how to successfully deal with these problems, then...

CHANGE OCCURS!

STEP SIX

Having a goal will raise your level of motivation. You know the process, but it's important to have a very clear goal. You can't just say, I want to lose weight. You have to be specific. CREATE YOUR OWN GOAL.

Make your goal specific. It doesn't have to cover everything you want to do. It is better to start with small goals that you can achieve.

Make sure that you can measure your goal. Can you say, "I can do it" ... and "I did it!"

Make your goal something that is acceptable to you. It must be tolerable and bearable to you. If you hate to swim, don't make your goal that you will swim two times a week!

Be realistic. Your goal has to be something you can achieve and fits into your present lifestyle. It's best to make it something that isn't difficult for you to achieve. If you want to lose 50 pounds, start by losing two pounds a week. Think about the two pounds, not the 50. Be realistic. There must be a beginning and an end to your goal.

The following are goals that are realistic.

I will walk for 30 minutes on Monday, Wednesday and Friday mornings after work.

I will eat only one sweet snack a day for the next two weeks.

I will drink only one soda every other day for the next month.

I will park at least six parking spaces further than I normally do from the grocery store for the next month.

I will spend 20 minutes on a relaxation technique every day after work for one week.

I will drink 7 glasses of water a day for the next two weeks.

Create your goal.

My GOAL _____

_____

_____

_____

_____

STEP SEVEN

Take time to understand and use this process. It will help to motivate you. Begin, by thinking about one change you would like to make. Be specific. Make it something you can measure: I will lose 20 pounds in four months. I will do an aerobic workout for 20 minutes two times a week. Complete your own chart.

MY PROBLEM/SITUATION

_____

_____

_____

_____

MY GOAL

_____

_____

_____

_____

WHY I WANT TO CHANGE

_____

_____

_____

_____

INFORMATION I NEED TO KNOW

_____

_____

_____

_____

HOW I WILL BENEFIT FROM THE CHANGE

_____

_____

_____

PROBLEMS THAT MAY ARISE

_____

_____

_____

_____

_____

CHANGE OCCURS! YOU WIN!

STEP EIGHT

If you think about your chance of success before you take on a change, you will increase your level of motivation. When you try something new, you've already decided whether you will succeed at it or not. You have most of the answers; you just may not recognize them.

Answer the following questions.

	(Low)				(high)
	1	2	3	4	5

I have the ability to make
this change.

I have the time to include
this change in my schedule.

I want to do it.

I need to do it.

Based on your answers, do you think you will succeed?

_____

_____

_____

STEP NINE

Certain techniques can motivate you. Here are some suggestions in case you are having difficulty sticking to your goal.

Choose one person who can be your "PAL." Keep in touch with him/her. Report your progress.

Ask him/her today. "I am going to change..... I need support. Can I call you?"

MY PAL
Email address_____
Telephone Number_____
Notes_____
_____
_____
_____
_____
_____
_____

Eliminate the defeatist attitude.

If you say you won't be able to complete your goal, you WON'T!
It starts in your head! Eliminate self-defeating thoughts and statements.

If you choose to make your goal a challenge, you will succeed.
WHAT YOU THINK IS WHAT YOU WILL ULTIMATELY DO...

"My goal can be challenging."
"I can do it."

Write two negative statements and transform them into two ways you can make change.

Negative Statements   CHANGE TO POSITIVE STATEMENTS:

_____
_____
_____
_____
_____
_____

STEP TEN

When you recognize what works best for you, it will add to your level of motivation. Rate each of the following techniques according to how helpful they are to you in reaching your goal.

	Not helpful at all		Very helpful	
	1	2	3	4	5
Working on my self esteem					
Planning a schedule					
Making a TO-DO list					
Recognizing my values					
Knowing more factual information					
Understanding how change works					
Getting support from friends					
Making a GOAL					

How confident do you feel that you will reach your goal?

1____2____3_____4_____5_____6_____7_____8_____9_____10
Not at all   Very confident

How much effort will you put into making sure your goal works?
1____2____3_____4_____5_____6_____7_____8_____9_____10
Not at all   Very confident

How difficult is it for you to maintain a goal that involves extra time and effort?
1____2____3_____4_____5_____6_____7_____8_____9_____10
Not difficult   Very difficult

CONGRATULATIONS! You're well on your way toward understanding who you are and how to achieve your goals. You're familiar with the process of change, and you know how to motivate yourself to improve your lifestyle.

Take it all in! Go for it! You have the skills necessary to make successful change, and you're on your way to a winning season!

MY PERSONAL GAMPLAN

THE FACTS ABOUT MY HEALTH

1. MY HEALTH

   How would you rate your health today? Place an X on the line.

   _____|_____

   Death – Disease – Unhealthy Lifestyle Awareness – Growth -Optimal health

2. SCREENINGS AND IMMUNIZATIONS YOU NEED

   Look at this list and then fill out your personal chart below.

	Age	Frequency
Blood cholesterol test	18-49	Once every 3 yrs
	50 & older	Yearly
Adult tetanus and diphtheria toxoid	18 yrs, & older	every10 yrs
Rubella titer test and immunization	18 yrs, & older	once
Influenza vaccine	50 yrs, & older	Yearly
Pneumococcal vaccine	65 & older	Once every 5 yrs.
Urinalysis	18 yrs, & older	Once every 3 yrs.
	50 & older	Yearly
Fecal occult blood test	50 years & older	Yearly
Complete blood count	18-49 yrs.	Once every 3 yrs.
	50 & older	Yearly
Flexible sigmoidoscopy or colonoscopy	50 & older	Yearly
Prostate-specific antigen	50 & older	Yearly for men
Mammogram	40 & older	Yearly for women
Routine gynecological exam & Pap smear	All ages	Yearly for women

INFORMATION I NEED TO KNOW:	Yes	No
Have you had your blood cholesterol taken in the past three years if you are between 18 and 49, or in the past year if you are 50 or older? * Your normal blood cholesterol should be under 200		
What is your overall Cholesterol? _____		
What is your HDL Cholesterol? _____		
What is your blood pressure? Normal is 120/80. _____		
Have you had an adult tetanus and diphtheria toxoid in the past ten years?		
Have you had a rubella titer test and immunization?		
If you are over 50, do you think you need an influenza vaccine?		
Does your doctor recommend that you get one? Have you had one?		
Have you had a urinalysis in the past three years if you are 18-49 or in the past year if you are over 50?		
Have you had a fecal occult blood test in the past year?		
Have you had a complete blood count in the past year?		
If you are over 50 have you had a flexible sigmoidoscopy or a colonoscopy?		

	Yes	No
Have you asked your doctor about the need to get one every five years?		
For men over 50, do you have a yearly prostate-specific antigen?		
For women over 40, do you have a mammogram yearly?		
For women, do you have a routine gynecological exam and Pap smear yearly?		
What is your heart rate? _____ (Normal- 72-80 beat per minute)		
What is your blood sugar? _____		
If you are under 50 years old, have you had a physical exam in the past three years?		
If you are over 50, have you had a physical exam in the past year?		

MY FAMILY HISTORY

Listed below are the leading causes of premature death in the United States. Which conditions do you or someone in your family have?

	ME	FAMILY MEMBER
CANCER		
HEART DISEASE		
HIGH BLOOD PRESSURE		
OBESITY		
STROKE		
DIABETES		
ARTERIOSCLEROSIS		
LUNG DISEASE		
LIVER DISEASE		
OTHER		

MY MEDICATIONS

List all of your medications. Take this book to the doctor with you.

PRESCRIPTION MEDICINES:

OVER THE COUNTER MEDICATIONS:

DIETARY SUPPLEMENTS:

VITAMIN SUPPLEMENTS:

HERBS:

OTHER:

QUESTIONS TO ASK AND TELL MY DOCTOR

Do I know all the medications I am presently taking?   Yes   No

Do my doctors know all of the other health professionals I see?   Yes   No

I am allergic to the following:

_____

_____

_____

_____

I take these medications for the following reasons:

_____

_____

_____

_____

How long should I take each of my medications?

_____

_____

_____

_____

What are the side effects of each medication?

_____

_____

_____

_____

Do I know the foods and drinks I should and should not take with my medications? List them.

_____

_____

_____

Do I read the labels on all of my medications?   Yes   No

Do I know how to measure my liquid medication?   Yes   No

Are my medications safe to take with other medicines? Yes   No

Information I need to consider:

_____

_____

_____

_____

3. MY MENTAL HEALTH AND VALUES

Look at the chart below, and think about how you feel about yourself.

	Little					Great				
	1	2	3	4	5	6	7	8	9	10
I feel good about myself										
Other people respect me										
I am worthwhile										
I am loved										
I feel valued										
I work on my self esteem										
I am assertive										
I have definite goals										
I know how to manage conflict										
I love to be challenged										
I have a purpose in life										
I am responsible										
People like me										
I know how to make decisions										
I feel successful										

Changes I would like to make:

_____

_____

_____

ABOUT ME

Put a T for True next to those statements that describe you and an F for False next to those statements that do not describe you. What do these statements tell you about yourself? What if they were all true or all false?

1. I am able to relax and enjoy myself.

2. I know my "purpose"–at least for today.

3. My work is important to me.

4. I wake up happy and energized in the morning.

5. I do not use phrases like "I hate...", "That's impossible,"... "I can't."

6. I empathize with those who have troubles greater than mine.

7. I like to be around happy people.

8. I try to laugh every day.

9. I use my imagination.

10. I know how to get things done.

11. I am not afraid to say I don't know something.

12. When I am confronted with a difficult situation, I know how to handle it.

13. I am persistent.

14. I can accept when I am wrong.

15. I am organized and can manage my time well.

16. I am an optimist.

17. I listen carefully when others speak to me.

MY VALUES

Look at the values listed below. Check the five most important to you. What do they tell your about yourself?

Health is a major concern.

I need to be in excellent shape.

My family is most important to me.

I need to be independent.

I want a big house.

I follow my religion and pray regularly.

I need to make a lot of money.

I need to have a job that is very exciting.

I need to be peaceful.

How I look is very important to me.

My community work is a major part of my life.

I need to be organized all the time.

Being well respected by my community is of utmost importance.

Being in a healthy relationship is tops on my list.

I need to be physically active a lot of the day.

I need to be in an academic community.

MY LIFESTYLE FACTORS

MY NUTRITION PLAN

_____

_____

_____

_____

_____

_____

_____

PHYSICAL EXERCISE

_____

_____

_____

_____

_____

_____

_____

MENTAL EXERCISE

_____

_____

_____

_____

_____

_____

_____

STRESS

_____

_____

_____

_____

_____

_____

_____

SLEEP

_____

_____

_____

_____

_____

_____

_____

ATTITUDE AND HAPPINESS

_____
_____
_____
_____
_____
_____
_____

BEHAVIOR HURDLES

TIME MANAGEMENT

_____
_____
_____
_____
_____
_____
_____

MOTIVATION

_____
_____
_____
_____
_____
_____

HOW I LOOK NOW

_____

_____

_____

HOW I FEEL NOW

_____

_____

_____

HOW I HOPE TO LOOK IN FIVE YEARS

_____

_____

_____

HOW I HOPE TO FEEL IN FIVE YEARS

_____

_____

_____

HOW I HOPE TO LOOK IN TEN YEARS

_____

_____

_____

HOW I HOPE TO FEEL IN TEN YEARS

_____

_____

_____

Life is a journey—
are you prepared to go
the distance?